Praise for *We* *Were Pretty Normal*

Get ready to go on a remarkable journey of what it looks like to watch your world shatter before your very eyes and be forced into a wrestling match with the fears and doubts that inevitably accompany us in our darkest times. Faith is more than a gift we're given; it's a tool we must exercise and use in order to experience its supernatural power. Michael Kelley poignantly illustrates the process of turning faith from a noun to a verb and how it can transform and shape our ability to persevere. Everyone needs to read this book.

—Pete Wilson, pastor and author of *Plan B*

A huge man and a tiny child walk hand in hand through these pages, then right out of the book and into your heart. Read it for your own edification, if you wish! But be alert! There are other parents you may not have noticed, who grieve quietly and are much afraid. Look hard, they're not usually out in the open, but they are there in the shadows of desperation. They need this book. Care! Then buy it for them. Then read them the first page and leave them alone. From that one page they will begin their own journey through Gethsemane. Then in the company of Michael and his Savior, their neediness will dissolve in wisdom.

—Calvin Miller, author and professor at
Beeson Divinity School

Many parents fear, often from the very first breath of a baby, that they will someday find themselves in a cancer ward with their beloved child. At first I resisted reading this book, afraid that it would be emotionally draining and gut-wrenching. I was wrong. This book will drive you to hope, joy, and trust in God's purposes, even if you find yourself where you feared you might be.

—Russell D. Moore, dean of
The Southern Baptist Theological Seminary

In the midst of a battle no one wants to face, Michael wrestled with issues about God and faith and the difficulty of life that many of us will confront in some way. Honest, heartbreaking but beating loudly with hope, *Wednesdays Were Pretty Normal* is a beautiful book.

—Jon Acuff, best-selling author
of *Quitter* and *Stuff Christians Like*

C. H. Spurgeon used to say that doubt was a foot poised to go forward or backward in faith. This book is an uncomfortably honest one that raises the foot. But throughout the story, Michael points back to a God that is deeper than the pain and doubts and guides us beyond Christian platitudes to genuine rest in the arms of our heavenly Father. I look forward to recommending this book to people in our church who can't seem to get an answer to the "why."

—J.D. Greear, lead pastor of The Summit Church in
Raleigh-Durham, North Carolina and author of *Gospel*

The Christian lives life between Earth and heaven, with one foot in each. Michael Kelley captures this dynamic well, taking the reader between sorrow and triumph, pain and joy. I feel very strongly that this story is one that must be shared again and again. You'll find yourself seeing faith, hope, and ultimately, God, in a much more intimate way than you have before.

—Mark Batterson, author pastor of National Community Church, Washington, DC

There are countless wildernesses: from depression to divorce, from brokenness to bankruptcy. For too many of us, cancer is our wilderness. Michael Kelley wandered that particular wilderness with his wife Jana as they watched and waited while their son Joshua wrestle with leukemia. I am sorry for their suffering. I am sorry for the time they lost that they will never get back. But I am deeply thankful that they did not waste their sorrow, and I am deeply thankful that Michael wrote this book.

—Michael Card, Christian singer/songwriter

A heart-breaking, thoughtful, and profoundly encouraging book written from real life experience. For everyone who has ever wondered why bad things happen, Michael's book doesn't answer the question. It does something better—it points all of us who know what it means to hurt to a God who is both passionately loving and still divinely sovereign.

—Ed Stetzer, vice president of LifeWayInsights

What a moving, honest memoir of real people facing the horrific nightmare of a life-threatening childhood disease! It pulsates with raw emotion, frank questions, and deep spiritual resolve. My friend, Michael Kelley, tells his family's story with transparency and authenticity. No sugar-coated, pseudo-spirituality here! Just the truth about finding God's grace in the midst of genuine pain. An inspiring story for all—a life-changing story for those who are facing a similar situation.

—Dr. Jeff Iorg, president,
Golden Gate Baptist Theological Seminary

Anyone who has ever had a sick child will find much needed words of comfort, encouragement, and a powerful reminder that you're not alone. Whether for yourself or your friends, you'll discover divine solace in these pages.

—Margaret Feinberg, author of *Scouting the Divine*
and *Hungry for God*

Michael Kelley is a gifted communicator and offers the church in this generation much promise. I am pleased not only to recommend this book, but also to commend this faithful servant of the Lord. These pages are filled with the life-changing experience of his son's cancer diagnosis and treatment. The relational and spiritual insights you'll read about are hard earned and precious. Michael pulls back the curtain on faith and hope during times of difficulty. He does so with honesty and transparency, allowing us to hear his questions and doubts and to feel the weight of the struggle alongside him. But he also gives us the chance to hear profound truths that God taught him in those moments—truths about God's character, purposes, and love.

—Thom S. Rainer, president and CEO of
LifeWay Christian Resources

Wednesdays Were Pretty Normal is not a "cute kid overcomes the odds" or sentimental story of suffering; it shows us the intersection of Christ's gospel with the realest of the real. With wit, insight, and power, Michael Kelley reveals the promises of God's Word found in the very wounds He allows. Joshua's story won't just move you; it will move you forward in your faith.

—Jared Wilson, author of *Your Jesus Is Too Safe* and
Gospel Wakefulness

You're asked to blurb a book—I assume—to bring something to the book, like credibility. But while reading Michael Kelley's book, I couldn't help but think I am the one being honored to associate myself with it. It presents the picture of a man both walking with God, like Enoch, and wrestling with God, like Jacob. It takes you down a road where love and tragedy and wisdom and hope all merge. It is a genuinely special book, at once deeply personal and transcendently godward.

—Jonathan Leeman, editorial director of 9 Marks

Parenting is a word that should make us all tremble. The daily joy comes with multiplied challenges for anyone blessed with the responsibility to lead and care for little lives. Anyone who knows Michael and Jana respects that for their family, parenting has taken their family on a journey face-to-face with leukemia, with too many needles, hospitals, and departures from the "normal" parenting journey. In *Wednesdays Were Pretty Normal*, Michael's "father" voice shares the difficulty of the most simple things like playing baseball and the joy of looking back to see that the journey has led them to the heart of Christ.

—Randy Hall, CEO of Student Life

Wednesdays Were Pretty Normal is about personal faith forged through the fire of suffering and the all-encompassing grace of a God who won't fit into the boxes we try to construct around Him. This is not a sentimental memoir or another theoretical look at suffering. Instead, Michael leads us to the intersection of faith and life, of God's love and our pain, of God's plan and our questions.

—Trevin Wax, editor of TGM (Theology, Gospel, Mission) at LifeWay Christian Resources, author of *Counterfeit Gospels* and *Holy Subversion*

Finally comes an approach to human crisis that debunks faith in faith and faith without fright. For Michael Kelley, untried and untested faith is not little faith—it is no faith at all. This work commends faith in the God of the Scriptures who both delivers and sustains in the midst of crisis. Michael is no armchair observer; instead he is an eyewitness who believes that one cannot get to the banquet table in Psalm 23:5 without going through the valley in Psalm 23:4.

—Dr. Robert Smith, Besson Divinity School

I sat down to skim this and instead read every word start to finish. Reader, please listen to me: If you have ever suffered, struggled, doubted, wrestled with a God who allows hunger and disease and two-year-old boys to get cancer, if you have attempted to believe God in the midst of devastation or fear, please devour this book like the gift it is. Thank you, Michael, for not only honestly sharing your story with us but drawing us deeper into the true, rich, genuine love of Jesus who cries with us, stays by us, and redeems us.

—Jen Hatmater, author of *7*

Wednesdays **were**
pretty normal

Wednesdays Were pretty normal

A boy, cancer, and God

Michael Kelley

PUBLISHING GROUP

NASHVILLE, TENNESSEE

978-1-4336-7169-2

Published by B&H Publishing Group

Nashville, Tennessee

Dewey Decimal Classification: 234.2

Subject Heading: CANCER \ FAITH \ SUFFERING

1 2 3 4 5 6 7 8 • 16 15 14 13 12

Dedication

To Joshua Michael, Andi Hope, and Christian Parker, who teach me every day both what it means to be a father and a child. I love you very much.

Acknowledgments

So many people have played an important role not only in this book, but in the story of the last several years of our lives. It is through these good people that I have filtered these events through the lens of faith, and for their constant support, affirmation, laughter, and tears I am indebted.

Jana, what can I say? My words always seem so paltry when stacked against the reality of who you are. You are a blessing to all who know you, and you are the most tangible expression of the grace of God in my life.

Gram, PaPaw, Nana, Papa, Cory and Kim, Brad and Amy, Eric and Jenni, and Jeffrey and Noelle—thank you for the standard of "family" that you have set. Through your examples of values, parenting, and grace we are continuing to learn about who Jesus is.

Thanks, too, to the staff of the fine Vanderbilt Children's Hospital. Your uncanny ability to make Joshua still look forward to his appointments at the clinic is baffling. Thank you for being the instruments of God who have, in truth, saved our son's life.

The people of Grace Community Church in Nashville, Tennessee—you have reminded us what church could be.

Your emphasis on grace alone through faith alone and your gospel-centered lives have inspired our imaginations and encouraged us to keep walking.

Finally, to "those people"—the ones that didn't leave. The ones who did our laundry, mowed our grass, bought your own containers of Purell, ate hot dogs with us in hospital waiting rooms, and a host of other little things, which neither we or the Lord Jesus will never forget. You have stood beside us in the trenches. You have looked the brokenness of humanity in the eye. And you did not back down. It continues to be a great and mighty privilege to link arms with you.

Contents

Chapter 1

Diagnosis

Joshua

My son likes his peanut butter and jelly sandwiches cut into long, thin strips. It's a little extra effort, but every time I make him a sandwich, I spread a thick layer of peanut butter on one piece of bread and an equally thick layer of jelly on the other. Then I mash the two onto each other, bringing together the classic blend of sweet and salty, and I cut off the crusts. I read somewhere that the crust is good for you, like the skin of potatoes, but Joshua doesn't like it. Even now at seven years old, he hasn't grasped the need for nutrition yet, and sometimes I count it a moral victory that he's getting in his fruit group from the jelly side, so I don't press the crust issue. Then I cut the sandwich into four long, thin pieces.

His name is Joshua Michael Kelley—not very original, I know. When he was born in 2004, *Joshua* was the third most popular name for boys in the United States; "Michael" was second most popular. No points to us for creativity.

But we didn't consult the lists for trendy names during those days. We named our first-born child "Joshua" for two reasons. First and foremost, we loved the name. We thought it inspired strength and conviction. We still hope the day never comes when his name gets shortened to "Josh"—I think that shortened version takes away from the power of the original. We wanted him to be named Joshua—the whole name, with the whole meaning. That's the second reason for our choice.

Joshua is a Jewish name, and while we have no physical Hebrew lineage, we resonate with the meaning: "the Lord is salvation." Being a family of faith, we enjoy the implication of the name and hope that someday he'll grow to appreciate it as well. We want Joshua to live a life in which he knows who God is and is confident in himself because he's confident in God. We don't necessarily expect him to be a tremendous scholar or someone of great prestige or fame (though watching my son play for the Atlanta Braves would be just fine with me). No angels came down out of heaven to make a grand prediction about his future. But we do want him to walk in confidence, knowing that God is salvation—nothing else. Even in hopeless times, God is salvation, regardless of what career or family track he chooses.

So that's the name we chose. We decorated his room in blue and red; we had a picture framed commemorating his name and the meaning behind it. And we expected to live happily ever after. In 2004 we imagined Joshua standing up for his moral convictions throughout his teenage years. I think we hoped that he would choose to believe rather than doubt as he made career and educational decisions. We did not, however, expect the reality of life to come crashing into our insulated world as quickly as it did.

PB & J

My wife, Jana, picked up Joshua from Parents' Day Out on October 17. That in itself was a little unusual because I usually picked him up. About eight months earlier we had made the decision to drastically alter our lifestyle. I loved to teach and write, and so we decided to make a go of my being an independently employed freelance communicator. Catchy job title, right?

I left my job working as a student pastor in Nashville, Tennessee, to try to make it happen. In true romantic fashion, Jana went back to work teaching fourth grade while I went to chase dreams. Our hope was that she would do this for two years until my work was steady enough for her to be a stay-at-home mom again for a while. In the meantime I would stay at home with Joshua and work during his naps and on the days he went to his preschool. That's why he was at Parents' Day Out rather than Mother's Day Out; I was too insecure to call it Mothers' Day Out since, well, I'm not a mother. But on this particular day, Jana was on fall break from her school, so I took that Tuesday to work all day while she had full Joshua duty.

After Jana picked him up from his day at school, we hit the park in downtown Nashville. Joshua still has a half-broken front tooth as a reminder of the day because I got a little too ambitious on a teeter-totter. As we scoured the ground around the playground looking for a miniscule piece of a two-year-old incisor, Jana mentioned that one of the workers at the day care had noticed a rash on Joshua's belly when she was changing his diaper. That was trouble because it violated one of the cardinal rules of day care: Don't send a sick kid to be around the well kids. Just to confirm it was nothing, I dutifully promised to take Joshua to the doctor the next day—always an interesting adventure for a dad.

The next day was Wednesday, October 18, and Joshua and I gathered up some trucks into his bag. We set out for Harpeth Pediatrics to get what I was sure would amount to some overly smelly cream that I would have to spread onto the trunk of his body for a week. While I didn't relish the thought of smelling like an old man with skin problems, I did like the idea of being

4

able to stride into the preschool and assure everyone that I had taken the appropriate steps to make sure Joshua was well. I made him a sandwich so we could have a picnic after the doctor's visit. I made it just the way he likes it. Peanut butter on one side, jelly on the other. Smash it together, and cut it into long, thin strips.

Cancer

It's not that difficult to tell when someone has something he needs to tell you but really doesn't want to—-you can almost always sense the news coming. It's the same feeling you have right before a news broadcaster interrupts the regularly scheduled programming for a special message. Or when your spouse is talking on the telephone to someone in grave, hushed tones, only to hang up and invite you to "have a seat. I have something to tell you." It's that feeling where you hold your breath without knowing it and you feel your heart beating inside your head.

Dr. Collins had ordered a blood test after examining Joshua; while the blood test came and went, I tried to keep a two-year-old preoccupied in the prison-cell-sized examination room. We played with trucks. Then we played with a lot of medical instruments that I'm sure we weren't supposed to touch. Joshua ate one strip of his sandwich. Then the doctor came back. He sat across from me. Looking at him, I subconsciously held my breath. My heart started beating in my head. Why was I nervous? We had been to the doctor before. But something was different this time. Then he started saying words that I never expected to hear: "hematology," "children's hospital," "call your wife." Then he said the word that would become part of our everyday vocabulary at heartbreaking speed: *leukemia*.

What do you do with a word like that? How do you respond? What questions do you ask? I didn't know; I still don't know. But I think I do know that some words in our vocabulary are heavier than others, words that linger in the air long after they are said. They echo in your mind and pierce your heart over and over again, and when they are first spoken, they drop to the pit of your stomach like lead. *Leukemia*.

Two hours later Joshua was still playing with his trucks, but he was playing with them on the floor of an examination room at Vanderbilt Children's Hospital. My wife had joined us, and we were waiting for the results of a secondary blood test they had done. We didn't speak. We didn't cry—much. We hoped, we tried to pray, we wanted to believe. And then we had another sit-down moment.

Amid Joshua's truck sound effects and laughter, we heard the confirmation that our two-and-a-half-year-old boy had a childhood cancer of the blood. And it felt as if someone had punched me as hard as they could in the gut. *Leukemia*. There was that word again, and there was the lead-heavy residue in the air. It echoed in my heart.

Over and over again the words punched. The emotion welled behind my eyes until I thought my head would explode. How could 82 percent of his blood cells be affected? He's playing with trucks! How could he have cancer? I made him a sandwich this morning! And it wasn't just the emotion that throbbed; it was the questions. So many questions that I didn't even know where to begin.

There were the questions you'd expect:

- Is Joshua going to die?
- How can he be sick? He looks fine!
- Isn't it just a rash?
- How do you treat leukemia?
- What does this mean about the future?

But then there were the other questions:

- Why this little boy, God?
- How could You let this happen?
- Is this punishment for something we have done?
- Are You even real?

Joshua finished his sandwich, and I started to cry. I cried because there he was, eating his strips of PB & J the same way he had hundreds of times before. And while he ate, I wondered how many more times he would.

Calls

In a span of moments that seemed like months, we had become "those people." You know those people—the ones with the sick kid. The ones with the terminal disease. The ones with "issues." The ones you don't get too close to, not because you don't care but because you don't want to think about what life would be like if that happened to you. You know, *those* people.

The worst part is that we were not those people—we were the people who were supposed to "be there" for those people. I went to seminary for crying out loud! I was a professional Christian! We were a family of faith who believed in Jesus and His way of life, and as such we prepared ourselves to counsel those people. We filled our spiritual tool bag with Bible verses and theological sayings. We practiced good eye contact and carried tissues in our pockets to give to someone else. In all of our preparation to be with those people, we never prepared to be those people ourselves.

But I guess nobody ever really does. Nobody is ever prepared for the weight of the words, for the suddenness of the diagnosis. And maybe that's why nobody really knows the right way to act when you become those people. But when you become those people, some things have to be done. Like, for example, making the phone calls.

Talk about being unequipped. I did not have the skill set

to talk to the grandparents. The aunts and uncles. The friends. I didn't have the emotional equipment. Heck, I didn't even have the informational equipment. I certainly didn't have the spiritual equipment, but the calls had to be made, and made they were. At great length I was able to articulate the diagnosis to both sets of our parents. The effort of squeezing those thousand-pound words out of my mouth made me gag several times, but after a long time in the courtyard of the hospital, I walked back inside to join my wife.

Beginning

I found her eating pizza. Can you believe it? Freaking pizza!

But here's the thing—she had to eat pizza; when Joshua was diagnosed, Jana was two months pregnant with our second child. I don't think either one of us realized how hungry we were until the sweet nectar of pork and cheese hit our lips, and we devoured what was in front of us. And then, in the middle of the feast, we started to laugh.

Truth be told, I'm not sure what it was that we laughed about, but something was funny and we laughed. And we laughed. Then we laughed more. I quoted a line from *Steel Magnolias* about laughter through tears; then we laughed at how ridiculous it was that I quoted *Steel Magnolias*. She made fun of me for my knowledge of chick flicks. I made fun of her for her inability to stop eating pizza.

The pizza helped a lot for some reason. Maybe it was a reminder that some things in life would still be stable and regular, like our need for food that's bad for us. We would still sleep, still work, still live. And as we settled down a little bit and the initial shock of how life had just changed started to sink in, I had time to start processing some of those questions we were just beginning to have.

What does one do—one who believes in the gospel of Jesus Christ and gets paid for speaking and writing to others about how to do so better—what does someone like that do with news like this? At least in part, I think the right answer is to believe. Have faith. But what I began to realize is that up to that point in my life, *faith* had largely just been a noun.

A condition. An emotion. A feeling. Something like that. But sitting there with greasy pizza fingers, I knew the noun wasn't going to cut it any more. I couldn't just sit there and have faith, like I could just sit there and grow fat off pizza. Faith had to become a verb. Having grown up in an upper-middle-class household, never facing any major disease, poverty, racism, or even shortage of money; having never been without work, never been without education, and never been without cause to believe that all those things would just be there tomorrow, I realized that faith had never been hard. It had never been work. But it surely was now.

All

But this was a moment when we couldn't just *have* faith; we had to *choose* faith. It had to be as conscious as any other decision; like choosing to exercise in the morning, faith needed to be discipline. And just like hauling yourself out of bed to go for a jog at 5:00 a.m., choosing faith was hard. Annoyingly hard. Frustratingly hard. But in its hardness, I also began to realize that I don't get the old adage that faith is a crutch for the weak to lean on.

That's what enlightened people say. They say that faith is for the weak minded and the heavy laden. They say that faith is for those who find their circumstances too difficult to face. So these weak-minded simpletons feebly turn to the idea that there is something more, someone more, out there with a grand design of the universe because the reality they are in is simply too much to bear. They can't accept that everything happens by chance, and they happen to be the victim of a cosmic lottery that hands down cancer to peanut-butter eating, truck-playing two-year-olds. They can't face reality so they believe.

I don't think so. In that moment it would have been much easier *not* to believe than to believe. See, if you choose to believe in the God of the Bible, the God of David and Abraham and Jesus and Paul, you have to believe everything about Him. You can't just pick and choose parts of Christian theology to take in and others to reject. To take God's love is also to take His justice; to take His compassion is also to accept His wrath. It's not like a cafeteria line where you can just take mac and cheese and key lime pie because that's what your appetite tells you to take. You also have to take the asparagus.

You see the problem just as I did. If my family was really going to choose faith, then we would have to come to grips with the fact that there are parts of God and His plan that at best we don't understand; at worst we don't even like. We could no longer pick and choose certain parts of our belief system; we had to embrace all of it.

As we picked through the pages of the Bible during those first days, some promises jumped off the page at us. Verses like Psalm 112:7: "He will have no fear of bad news; his heart is steadfast trusting in the Lord" (NIV). Or the well-worn favorite Romans 8:28, where Paul reminds us that God "works all things for the good of those that love Him and are called according to His purpose" (NIV). We wanted to believe those verses. Badly. But the problem was that we feared bad news. Daily. Hourly. We were very much afraid. And Romans 8:28 felt like a pill that good Christian people were trying to shove down our throats. It's not that we doubted the truth of those verses; it was simply that we didn't see or feel how our pain was matching up to them. So began the collision of those well-worn Bible passages with our real-life experience. In my spirit, if not out loud, there was always a pause when I read a passage of hope.

I was crying out almost constantly for the reconciliation of what I believed to be true with what I was experiencing.

I remember clearly feeling that collision on one particular instance regarding one particular psalm, and I was both gratified and disturbed to see that this psalm acknowledged the inherent difficulty of our situation. Psalm 46:10a reads: "Be still, and know that I am God" (NIV). Now that's a great verse. In the chaos of blood tests and diagnoses, we would have loved nothing more than just to be quiet. Not just verbally, but in our minds and hearts, too—to calm down and just trust. Unfortunately, we couldn't. But then again, neither could the psalmist.

The psalm starts with encouraging words: "God is our refuge and strength, a helper who is always found in times of trouble. Therefore we will not be afraid, though the earth trembles and the mountains topple into the depths of the sea, though its waters roar and foam and the mountains quake with its turmoil" (Ps. 46:1). That's a pretty good description of what those moments feel like when you have to choose faith. Everything that just moments before you would have considered unshakable starts shaking. You want to emotionally crawl under a table or stand in the doorway in the midst of your circumstantial earthquake because the things of greatest strength, the things of most stability, the mountains and the earth and the oceans are falling down. But God, the most stable thing of all, is your help. He is ever present. He is not absent even in times of trouble. That is, He is safety; He is security; He is a place to hide from the elements outside, the destination to run to when no one else will take you. He is your refuge.

The image of a "refuge" is found throughout the Bible. Sometimes it's a high place, safe from threatening armies. Other times the word describes a city that is set up for all the greatest sinners to go to when no one else will take them. In still other verses the "refuge" is a cave to hide in to escape the elements of nature. Ultimately a refuge means that no matter what's going on outside, no matter what circumstances threaten, no matter how hard the wind and rain blow, no matter how bad the cancer is, no matter how bleak the job market seems, no matter how far gone the marriage might be, there is a place to come that is secure. And, according to this passage, the place to come is not really a place at all but a Person.

Surely the Lord is big enough to provide shelter from all the disease, all the shattered dreams, all the pressure, all the expectations the world can throw at us. After all, we see in Psalm 46 that when the mountains are giving way and the earth is falling into the heart of the sea, when the very basis of all visible things is being picked up and thrown about and the firmest of created things are being destroyed, our response should be simply *Selah*.

You can see that word at the end of verse 3. It appears

throughout the psalms as well as other places like Habakkuk 3. Though there is some discrepancy over its exact meaning, most agree that its effect is a pause. Silence. It is the moment when the music ceases in the psalm because what has just been said is so weighty that it bears a moment of further reflection. These are dire circumstances in Psalm 46, the circumstances of real life—those that make us doubt if God is real and if He is really active in our lives. Yet there is safety no matter how hard the wind blows or the mountains crash. There is security in God. The turmoil of the world is represented in the psalm by the ocean that is in an absolute uproar because of the mountains toppling into it. Another kind of water is mentioned, too—a river. A river that brings peace and gladness and life to all it touches. That's what God is like to the psalmist.

In the river we find peace. We find safety. We find God, and we can be still. And that's why the psalm closes with the directive that it does. Despite the circumstances, no matter what happens to the mountains or the seas, God is still God. No matter what happens in your son's bloodstream, God is still God. Be still. *Selah.*

Here's the problem though. It's not just that the mountains are quaking, that the earth is giving way. That the seas are roaring. That everywhere around us there is instability and destruction. The problem is that the language the psalmist uses is not coincidental; it's judgment language. It is virtually the same language the minor prophets used to describe the coming judgment of the nations. Judgment is not coincidental, nor is it random. It is a thought-out, well-planned, intentional act by God Himself.

The psalmist says as much down in verses 7 and 8. In verse 7 he affirms our greatest comfort that the Lord Almighty is with us; the God of Jacob is our fortress. But in the next verse he confirms what we fear; "Come, see," he says, "the works of the LORD, who brings devastation on the earth." That throws a wrench into the nice concept of God's being a refuge because He's not only what we run to but what we run *from*. These circumstances—the mountains crumbling and the seas foaming—are not just happenstance. They are not just casual incidents. They are the works of the Lord. Those circumstances in our lives that make us feel as though we need a refuge are, at best, allowed to be there by the Lord and, at worst, caused directly by Him. He may be our refuge, but it seems He is also our tormentor.

That's the reality of God's role in our lives. Even though He is our refuge, He is also the cause of our trouble. Some would go so far as to say that there is nothing in the universe that God does not directly control, whether winning the lottery or having a car crash. Others would say that He simply allows some things to happen—the bad things. But in the end the result is the same. In taking God as our refuge, we must also realize that these circumstances are in our lives because He has seen fit for them to be there. That's the whole truth.

Isn't that the definition of *cruelty*? Isn't that proof positive that our worst fears are true, that God doesn't really love us and that all of our doubts have substance? The picture seems to be one of a heartless deity who plays with underlings like ants, blocking their path with an object only to fry them with a magnifying glass when they look for another route. And that's the uncomfortable part of choosing faith.

That was the beginning of our journey with the Lord. It continues to be a journey with a lot of questions and not a lot of answers. The best we could muster were mere observations for the way things are rather than explanations of *why* things are the way they are. It is a journey of hospitals and treatments, of medication and addiction, of joy and pain. It's a journey of trying to embrace the fact that God is our refuge but not a comfortable one to hold onto. It's a journey of realizing that He is our safe place, and yet He is not safe at all. It's a journey of realizing more and more of what it means to walk deeply with God and all the doubt, fear, anxiety, peace, and joy that come with it and how those things can possibly coexist together. It's a journey of understanding that there is nothing like pain to force long-held ideals and beliefs from the comfort of intellectualism into the discomfort of reality and trying to square with them there.

Maybe you know what it feels like, too, to struggle with things that are too big for you to understand and yet to sense that this is the path God has chosen for you. And because He did, you keep going. You walk. You put one foot in front of the other.

And so we checked into the hospital. Joshua was to begin chemotherapy the next day. Apparently there was no time to lose.

Chapter 2

Doubt

Faith

Looking back on it, I think the day Joshua was diagnosed was the day I really became an adult. Ironic, since I was married and had a kid, but in some ways I was still functioning like a child. But in that moment I had no choice but to grow up. To quit being so selfish. To start thinking about my family for a change. And to begin to figure stuff out. Trust me. There was plenty to figure out. There were the immediate needs like the fact that we were suddenly in the hospital and we needed toothbrushes. And pajamas. And toys for our son. Not to mention the fact that Jana would have to be away from work, which was our steady source of income and health insurance. And where did that insurance fit in? Up to that point the words *premium* and *co-pay* were just nebulous, theoretical ideas out there for someone else to worry about. Now I had to figure out what they meant. And about that income—was there going to be enough money for everything that lay ahead? And while we're on that subject, what exactly did lay ahead? Everything in our lives had been thrown off kilter, and with everything up becoming down so quickly, you can imagine that we felt a loss of equilibrium. We felt dizzy in those practical aspects of life, but we also felt it spiritually.

While we were asking all those questions about the practical nature of having a kid in the hospital, we entered into another set of questions. We couldn't help but ask what this "faith" was that we so desperately wanted to hang onto. We didn't want to doubt, much less renounce, the timeless truths we believed: that God is good, that He is all powerful, that He chooses at times to heal and at times not to hear, and that He is always right and loving in His choice. But it became imperative for us to figure out what faith really looked like in our now inverted world. Sure, it was hard. Faith was a choice, that much we suddenly knew, but what were we trying so hard to do? What were we trying so hard to walk in? What does real faith look like?

Coming to the knowledge that you thought you knew something inside and out and then figuring out you really don't know it at all is a strange feeling. I remember having the same feeling just after I married Jana. I saw the way she fixed her cereal, how she cut her chicken, her morning routine of getting ready, the way she applied her makeup. And I remember thinking, *I really don't know this person at all.* So weird, especially considering that I was so sure that I did know her, that I did love her, and that I knew exactly what to expect.

Checking into the hospital and mulling over this "faith" that I was so sure I knew, so sure I loved, and so positive I believed produced similar feelings. Did I even really know the thing I was struggling to cling to with white knuckles?

What is faith? What does it mean to believe? Up to that point part of me had implicitly defined faith more in terms of what it is not rather than what it is. So for me, faith was *not* doubting. It was the absence of questions. It was following obediently without hesitation.

You see the obvious problem as clearly as I did. That definition of faith works great as long as everyone's healthy, there's plenty of money in the bank, and the cars are running. But if faith is the absence of doubt, where does that leave you when all you have is doubt? If faith is not asking the questions, then where does that leave you when all you have is questions? If faith is absolute certainty, then where does that leave you when nothing is certain anymore?

As I have so many times since that day, I flipped through the pages of my Bible not really knowing what I was looking for. A definition? A clarification? Or maybe something just to make me feel better about my single twine of belief that was enabling me to put one foot in front of the other? Maybe what I was really looking for was, selfishly, some evidence that God was not mad at me for barely hanging on. What I found was not a definition but a story.

Story

That's pretty appropriate, I guess. G. K. Chesterton once commented that he first and foremost saw all of life as a story. So is the Bible for that matter. Obvious stories appear in Joshua's read-along children's Bible, the ones that conveniently leave out the death and destruction of Noah's ark and the beheading of David's Philistine. But even beyond those, all of Scripture is really a story. Even those passages that are didactic in nature are still a story. There's a story behind Paul's instructions to Timothy. There's a story behind why Peter wrote about persecution and why James talked about equality. Everything is a story, and I found a story in Mark 9.

Conveniently, this story involved a father and a son, and in some ways, I felt a lot like the dad I read about. Here, too, was a guy hanging on by a thread and, more than anything in the world, was just looking for his boy to get better. That fit, so I read on:

"Teacher, I brought my son to You. He has a spirit that makes him unable to speak. Wherever it seizes him, it throws him down, and he foams at the mouth, grinds his teeth, and becomes rigid. So I asked Your disciples to drive it out, but they couldn't." (Mark 9:17–18)

If you skip down a few verses, you see the continued exchange between Jesus and the dad:

"So they brought him to Him. When the spirit saw Him, it immediately convulsed the boy. He fell to the ground and rolled around, foaming at the mouth. 'How long has this been happening to him?' Jesus asked his father. 'From childhood,' he said. 'And many times it has thrown him into fire or water to destroy him. But if You can do anything, have compassion on us and help us.'" (Mark 9:20–22)

There in the hospital I looked around and paused to think a little deeper about the situation this dad found himself in. My own circumstances gave me at least a little insight into his world and the ability to read between the lines of his request.

Details

I had to admit it—Vanderbilt Children's Hospital was pretty nice. The elevator took us to the sixth floor hematology ward, a place where Joshua could spend hours. There he was, on his first day in the hospital, lying on a bed in an elevator with people around him, trying to keep a mask on his face to keep out hospital germs, terrified. But when he finally looked up, he got calm.

"It's a duck!" came the garbled words from behind his mask. And sure enough, on the ceiling of the elevator was a three-dimensional duck with stars and stripes flying around him. A duck! He giggled and calmed down some more and for the next several hours wanted to ride the "duck-a-vator again." That was just the tip of the iceberg for Children's Hospital. Brightly painted, cheerful, and homey are a few of the ways that I would never think of to describe a hospital wing, and yet there it was. Toys in the hallways, kids walking around in pajamas, doors open, parents conversing with one another, nurses smiling at us as we walked by. Yet in the parents' eyes something was different. It wasn't pity necessarily; instead, I think it was an undercurrent of sadness—sadness about lost time, lost dreams, and lost expectations. They weren't just sad for themselves, either; they were sad for us, too, because they knew we had just become "those people." They were able to look at us and see that our journey had just started.

The paperwork was the first step, and after hours of explanations about menus, regulations for health and safety, and medical regiments, we went with Joshua out into the hallway to wander around his new temporary home. Much to our surprise, we heard laughter. Kids were playing baseball in the hallways. Sounds of movies and PlayStations firing came from almost every room. You could almost believe that we had stepped into some kind of righteous summer camp for rich kids where a staff waited on them hand and foot. Almost.

Just when you got a little engrossed in the camp illusion, you looked around with the renewed sense that this was no camp at all. The kids had no hair. Most were walking accompanied by an IV pole. Many had feeding tubes attached to their noses. And they got tired quickly. So quickly.

I think that's when I really started to identify with the other dad, the one in Mark 9, because I had the sensation that we would still do regular things—eat, drink, sleep, go to work, watch TV, and the other stuff of real life—but that all of those activities would be planned and dictated by what was wrong with my boy. That's what life must have been like for him, too.

Backstory

So I wondered: *What led that father to the base of the mountain that day so long ago? What was his backstory?* The dad claimed to Jesus that his son had been in this state since childhood, which indicates that maybe he was not a child anymore. Perhaps his son had passed the age of thirteen, the traditional coming-of-age moment in Jewish culture. If so, the son was now an adolescent, meaning that this affliction had followed them everywhere for years like an ever-present IV pole that tangles your feet when you're trying to run and gets in the way when all you want to do is work a puzzle.

The father from the story must have felt that too—that his life as well as his son's were centered around this illness. And as he made the request of Jesus, the pictures must have flooded through his mind: all the times when they were having dinner with friends and their son tipped the food bowls over with his shaking; the days when everything was normal until he looked out of the house only to see his son lying once again in the dirt; all the times he had held his son's head close to his chest as he cried because all the other little boys were making fun of him.

In a culture that looked at disease and misfortune as a curse from the Lord, perhaps the father's business had suffered, too. Maybe he struggled to find work because no one wanted to do business with the community pariah. And maybe even his relationship with his wife had gone south. Surely there was no time for intimacy between them when they had to keep constant watch on their son. How many nights had they tied him to his bed to make sure he didn't get up? How many conversations had been interrupted by his screaming? How many times had each of them stormed out of the house, not because they were frustrated with each other but because they just had to be somewhere different?

In coming to the mountain that day, I wonder if he really believed Jesus could do anything, or if he came with low expectations. Surely this was not the first "healer" he had approached to help his son. It certainly wasn't his first experience with disappointment. Maybe all he had was just the fleeting thought, the dream behind his eyes, that this time would be different. But it looked like he would be disappointed in this rabbi as well. After all, when he got there, Jesus wasn't even around. And when He finally did show up, He wasn't compassionate to the situation at all—He was frustrated. When Jesus saw the situation at hand and heard the man's sob story, He reacted by saying, "You unbelieving generation! How long will I be with you? How long must I put up with you? Bring him to Me." But let's cut Jesus some slack, too, because He had a lot on His mind.

The reason He wasn't there to begin with was because He was up on the mountain with three of His disciples experiencing something incredible. Jesus, Peter, James, and John were on the Mount of Transfiguration. Before the eyes of those three trusted disciples, Jesus was transfigured into something glorious. They saw Him as the Son of God, in whatever form that really takes. And not only that—Moses and Elijah showed up for the party, too. The three talked about various things but mainly focused on the impending climax of Jesus' ministry— His coming death, resurrection, and departure from the world. The parallel account in the book of Luke says literally that the three were discussing the "exodus," something all three had in common. Moses led the children of Israel out of slavery in an exodus. Elijah experienced his own exodus as he was taken up from the earth in a chariot of fire. And Jesus? Well, Jesus was going to do both—the children of God would be led on an exodus out of sin and death, and then Jesus would be taken up into heaven after His resurrection. The scene was apparently so amazing that Peter offered to set up some shelters on the mountain so they could all stay there.

But they couldn't. While the unreal was becoming real on top of the mountain, the pain of Earth was invading the valley. The dad and the son had found the other disciples. He had brought his boy to see Jesus, the mysterious but undeniably powerful rabbi, but had found a few of His followers instead. But they were better than nothing, right?

The other disciples tried to help but to no avail. What made the situation even more uncomfortable was that a crowd began to gather around the boy on the ground. Among the crowd were the teachers of the law, and quickly a squabble broke out between them. The religious authorities were sure they knew how to perform exorcisms, and they saw these failing attempts by the disciples as an opportunity for humiliation:

"You're not doing it right!"

"Yes we are!"

"Haven't you performed an exorcism before?"

"Of course we have; just give us some room!"

And so the situation worsened until the boy became an afterthought. Everyone seemed more concerned about being right than the boy, and for the father the thought of his son becoming little more than the centerpiece of a theological argument was too much to bear. Just as he was ready to pack in his hopes and tears, Jesus appeared. And no wonder Jesus was frustrated—just look at the situation!

Jesus had just been reflecting on His death—something that required an extreme amount of faith for even Him—and here He comes down to find everyone in unbelief. No one had faith down in the valley—not the teachers of the law who disbelieved the identity of Jesus, not the disciples who had lost their confidence, and especially not this pathetic man who couldn't begin to grasp the nature of the one he sought.

That's right—pathetical because not even this guy, who was in the most need of anyone at that moment, could muster up enough faith to believe. That really hit home for me. It was uncomfortably familiar to my own situation, and sitting there in the hospital room I came to the conclusion that God must be incredibly frustrated with me, too. My prayers for Joshua were tainted with doubt, and they sounded all too much like this man's request.

But at least that father was honest: "If you can do anything, take pity on us and help us." *If.* Now there's another weighty word with thousand-pound implications. With that one word, the man testified that he was no better than the less-than-confident disciples. *If. If* You are able. *If* You are loving. *If* You are who people say You are.

If. For the first time in my life, I had reason to say the word, too. And though I might not have been saying it outwardly, it was certainly lurking there below the surface. It betrayed my doubt and fear with its presence.

Despite the *if,* the father pleaded with Jesus. Literally he said, "Be moved in your bowels." Not a pleasant thought to us; but for the Jewish people at that time, the bowels were considered the deepest part of a person, the emotional center. "Be moved in your guts, in the deepest parts of who you are."

But Jesus turned the tables on the man. Maybe on me, too.

If

"If you can?" said Jesus. "Everything is possible for him who believes. The question, dad, is not whether I can. *I can.* Believe Me, I can. No, the question is actually more about you than it is Me. It is not about My ability; it is about your faith. *Do you really believe I can?"*

I didn't like that. I didn't like it because I couldn't emotionally or spiritually handle the pressure of thinking that the prognosis of my son's leukemia sat on my shoulders, that God was looking at *me* asking *me* about *my* faith. I couldn't handle it, not when I knew that everything I believed was hanging by a thread, precariously close to breaking. If . . . if only I did truly believe, Jesus. But I knew I did not. Not fully. Not wholly. Not after the morning I'd had.

And neither did the father. But this is where he and I are different. My tendency when my faith is less than perfect is to hide it. To act like I do believe. In fact, I have encouraged countless people to push doubt out of their minds and focus on their beliefs; in a way I have counseled others to be dishonest with God and with one another. I implicitly have said, "Say it until you believe it." But not this man. Rather than trying to find the perfect prayer, he said exactly what he felt. Exactly what he knew. Exactly what he believed, or in his case, what he didn't believe.

"I do believe; help my unbelief." Some ancient texts of this passage say that he said this through his tears. In an emotional outburst the man actually owned up to his doubt. How pathetic. How undignified. How unspiritual. How . . . honest.

And then the impossible happened. Jesus healed his son. Just like that. After years of struggle, countless tears, and immeasurable heartbreak and frustration, it was all done. The miraculous happened, but in the wake of that tremendous event, I have to wonder, *Why?* After all, Jesus asked for faith, and instead He got doubt. The man clearly did not meet the qualification for his son's healing. So why did Jesus do it?

Maybe it was because He's Jesus. He was so overcome by the depth of this man's emotion that it is as if He said; "It's true that you do not have enough faith for Me to do this. But it's obviously important to you, and lucky for you, I am Jesus after all. So out of My goodness, I will make an exception in your case and grant your request. But make sure you have more faith the next time you come to see Me." Maybe that's what happened. Or maybe Jesus looked around at the scene, the crowd, and decided it was time to end this whole thing because it was getting out of control. So He healed the kid almost out of frustration, just to be done with the matter.

But maybe, just maybe, Jesus saw in this man the very thing that He did not see in the teachers of the law and even His own disciples. Maybe Jesus found exactly what He was looking for in the man's emotional outburst. Maybe in the father's confession of his faithlessness, Jesus found the faith He had been looking for all along.

Maybe the difference between this guy and most of us is not the state of circumstances around us; we all have cancer or car wrecks or poverty or whatever. Maybe the difference is that this dad had the faith to doubt. Can that be right? This father had the faith to doubt? We have this idea of what faith must be, and that definition of faith has no room for doubt; no room for questioning. Who can blame us? After all, faith is being sure of what we hope for and certain of what we do not see, according to Hebrews 11:1. That's the definition of *faith* in Scripture.

And yet the people the writer of Hebrews holds up as examples of this kind of faith had questions and doubts. Abraham wondered how God could possibly make a couple so old have a son. Jacob had so little confidence in the promises of God that he tried to physically trap God into blessing him. Joseph was not content to wait on the plan of the Lord but took matters into his own hands to secure his release from prison. And yet these people are commended for their faith.

What if our definition of *faith* is wrong? What if we have been putting faith in our own ability to have faith? What if real faith is not necessarily absent of questions and doubt; what if real faith is more about what we *do* with doubt than whether we have it?

Questions

I looked at Joshua a lot in those days. I watched him sleep. I watched him watch videos. I watched him bravely take his medicine and try to adjust to life in a hospital cell. And I dreamed about what might happen in the future. I thought about him going on his first date. I thought about him getting his driver's license, getting married, and having a family of his own. But I also thought about other things that would have to happen in the future.

For example, I thought about how in six years or so I will have to have a certain difficult conversation with Joshua. At some point Joshua is going to want to know where babies come from. (What?! From the stork, of course!) It will be an excruciatingly awkward conversation filled with terms he won't understand. I'll probably use a diagram. But in the end, even though the conversation will be tough, I hope he actually asks me about it. I hope I don't have to bring it up to him. Because if he is willing to ask me about it, he is confident in our relationship.

If he is willing to ask me about it, he trusts me. He trusts me with his limited understanding. He trusts me with the awkwardness. He trusts me more than his own ability to comprehend everything I will tell him. And I will know he trusts me—that he has faith in me—not because he has no questions, but because he is willing to come to me honestly with his questions. In the coming we find faith.

That's what I learned from this dad whose son Jesus healed. I did not learn how to have a perfect faith. I learned that real faith is not necessarily the absence of doubt; it's about coming to Jesus with what you have. In honesty. Admitting where you fall short. And yet when you come, even though you don't meet the "requirements," you acknowledge something about the One you are coming to. You say that He is bigger than your questions. He is bigger than your unbelief. He is bigger than doubt.

That, friends, is where the gospel enters our prayers. The incredible news regarding faith is that from start to finish, God is in the business of making up for what we lack. And we lack much. In a base sense we lack anything that could possibly merit the love of God, and yet in the cross Jesus makes up for what we lack.

That pattern doesn't stop once we enter into relationship with the Lord either. It's amazing and glorious to think about the fact that even now, in the middle of our doubt and fear, Jesus Himself lives to intercede for us at the right hand of the Father. He's praying for us right now. And in those moments when we don't know what or how to pray, the Holy Spirit intercedes for us with deeper, more emotional, and more pure groanings and pleadings than we can possibly understand.

How astounding to consider that when we pray, we enter a conversation about us already going on among the members of the Trinity. Given that, what's left for us is simply to come and pray. To be honest with God—good, bad, and ugly included. We come to Jesus not as we can't but as we can. Not as we aren't but as we are. And we believe that Jesus can make up for all that we lack.

And so, in the hospital room that night, I did not believe. And yet I *really* believed, maybe for the very first time.

Chapter 3

Medication

―⟨―

Waiting Room

There is nowhere on Earth like a hospital waiting room. Most people have been in one at one time or another—waiting because your appendix is bursting, waiting because your kid has a gash that needs to be sewn up, waiting because a friend has been in surgery and you are holding vigil for her recovery. You wait. You wait alongside the smell of stale coffee, of Maury Povich on the hanging television with the "Do not change channel" sign on it, of the pacing, bleary-eyed occupants clamoring for a doctor's update.

We spent plenty of time in the waiting room. Though Joshua spent more than his share of time in a hospital bed, we also got to spend a lot of time at home. After the initial two or three weeks in the hospital, we were allowed to do his chemotherapy on an outpatient basis. But there were caveats to that freedom.

One of the unfortunate aspects of chemotherapy—along with the nausea, hair loss, and general awful feelings—is that chemo is an indiscriminate killer. The medicine attacks good cells as well as bad. And the intense regimen of medicine left Joshua susceptible to disease because along with fighting the cancerous cells, it broke down his fighter white blood cells, too. So wherever we went, we armed ourselves with two things: Purell, for excessive washing of hands in an effort to keep away germs, and a thermometer. We had the thermometer under the strict instructions that if Joshua ever got a fever that reached 100.5, we were immediately to come to the emergency room because of his low tolerance for disease. A fever could signal an infection, and because Joshua didn't have the strength to fight infection, it could be really dangerous. So we spent a lot of nights rushing to the hospital, only to sit for a few hours in the waiting room.

In the waiting room you sit alongside people of every race, culture, and economic background. You wait there together. This place—though full of grief, hardship, and anxiety— might be the closest place on Earth to the kingdom of God. In the waiting room all the things that separate people from one another tend to drift away. Somehow, in that small, glass-enclosed space, you don't seem so different from people of different nationalities. Or different social circles. Or different styles of dress. Or different languages. You hold one thing in common with everyone in that room—pain.

The pain takes different forms. For some it's actual physical pain. For others it's the emotional pain of watching someone close to them suffer. But pain unifies every black, white, brown, or otherwise colored person in that room. Indeed, pain is the common denominator of all humanity.

Regardless of where you come from, how insulated your lifestyle, how stable your finances, or how healthy your habits, you will have a moment in the waiting room. And in that moment none of that other stuff seems to matter very much. Everyone hurts in one way or another. The question is what you do with that pain.

Morphine

Sometimes the pain is physical; that's mostly what it was for Joshua. Jana and I have often thought of the blessing of having a child diagnosed with a disease like leukemia so young. At two years old, he wasn't able to grasp the emotional complexity of the situation. And, because he wasn't yet involved in things like sports, band, or school, he didn't experience the loss of those things. How much more difficult must it be for a teenager, in the throws of pubescent popularity contests and efforts to prove themselves academically or athletically, suddenly to be whisked away to a hospital room. How much more difficult for a parent to watch a child's self-esteem fade away with each strand of falling hair because of chemotherapy. It's not that way for a two-year-old. Joshua didn't experience the same sense of loss an older child or adult must feel.

Nevertheless, a young child with leukemia has his own set of challenges. Up until that point, the greatest pain Joshua had experienced was during an unfortunate incident when I left a hot barbeque grill lid laying on the patio. He thought it looked like something fun to touch, and that's a lesson you only have to learn once. But now? In the hospital? He was experiencing real physical pain. The dull ache of a hurting stomach. The discomfort of none of your clothes fitting right because your body is retaining water. The sensation of always having hair that once was firmly attached to your head falling into your food. And then there were the sores.

The toxic cocktail of drugs Joshua took orally began to cause extremely painful mouth sores. Because of his low white blood cell count, his body couldn't repair the damage quickly. So the sores lingered, day after day. The medicine had the same effect on the other end, forming sores on his bottom even though we tried to change his diapers as quickly as possible to keep his excrement away from his skin.

What made matters worse was that Joshua had to be on

a cycle of steroids in combination with his treatments. I kept waiting for him to rip his shirt off and start turning green, but the primary side effects we saw with this type of medicine were a combination of emotional and physical changes. On the emotional side everything was heightened. In an instant he could go from hugging and kissing you all over your face to throwing a blistering fit of rage because Barney's "Puppy Love" wasn't on television. Physically the steroids made him hungry—ravenously hungry—like three breakfasts at a time hungry.

When you take a medically induced, insatiable appetite and combine it with unhealing and painful mouth sores in a two-year-old, you've got a problem. All of that mixed together for a hurting little boy and a set of parents who could do little more than lie beside him in bed and stroke his head as he cried. The solution from the hospital was a morphine drip.

So the kind nurses on the sixth floor attached a bag of liquid morphine to Joshua's IV pole, his constant companion in those early days. And when he needed it, Jana or I could push a button that would cause a drip of the medication to enter into his fluids. We were encouraged to push the button liberally. We did. For Joshua's part that medication helped his pain. It didn't make it go away, but it dulled it for a while. In a sense the medication made him temporarily forget about the pain going on inside of him. Such is the case with all medication, whether morphine or something else.

Escape

We had no emotional morphine drip, there was no psycho-logical button we could press. But I found myself needing to forget, too. I found myself needing—*needing*—to escape the pain of the present circumstances. I expect I'm not alone in that need.

Do we turn to alcohol because it tastes good? Do we cheat on our spouses purely out of lust? Do we become addicted, entrapped, and unfocused purely out of desire? Or are we just trying to have the same experience a child can have, if even for a few moments, when a drip of a drug can help us forget about reality?

In the absence of emotional morphine, we turn to other means to help with our pain. These may be substances, but they can also be seemingly benign forms of medication. Take, for instance, a job. When things aren't going well at home, when a wife grows cold and distant, when a man's children refuse to respect and listen to him, the best and easiest way to forget about that reality is to forge himself a new one at the office. There he can be valued. He can be listened to. He can be important. He can escape.

Or maybe this one—when a woman looks around one day and finds that her life is slipping away, when she realizes that she's spent decades doing the same thing and yet has nothing to show for it, when she feels stuck behind car and house payments, then the easiest way to forget about that reality is to escape into fantasy. Pornography, online dating, and extra marital affairs are readily accessible to serve that need.

Or consider this—a man might be completely moral and totally "Christian." And yet his world is crumbling around him. So he throws himself into church activity after church activity, leading one Bible study and prayer meeting after another, and yet he never confronts the pain he's running from. Church can be medication, too.

We are, in fact, masters at medicating our pain. And all of these things—whether church, pornography, or drugs—can easily serve the greatest need in the moment—escape. That's what medication does. It doesn't take away the pain. It doesn't ultimately change the circumstances. It doesn't alter reality. But it does, however briefly, allow the pain of reality to be dulled. We don't have to think and feel what's really going on. Medication allows us to escape from reality; it keeps us from having to ask the difficult "what if" and "why" questions of our lives. If the common denominator of humanity is pain, then a valid question we must ask is what we do with that pain. Most of us are trying to escape, even if it's just for a while. I did it. I do it. But there is another option. It's a more difficult way, but nevertheless it is the way to approach something akin to healing. And that's pressing in.

Conflict

Medicate, or press in. Anyone who has heard the diagnosis, gotten the call from the police, been served the papers, or simply watched the devastation around the world can identify with that kind of choice. I sensed the choice laid out clearly before me. It was a choice about whether to push the emotional medication button, or press in, knowing that walking away from medication is tantamount to inviting the full measure of pain and struggle into the forefront of an already bruised heart. But struggle with whom? With the world? The disease? With Satan?

It's easier in moments of pain, when the questions invade your reality, to direct your sorrow, disappointment, and anger at Satan or a broken world or random occurrence. It's easier to let the blame lie there, but if we do, we are robbing God of His power and control and cheating ourselves out of fully processing the magnitude of who He is. Some would argue that God causes hardship. Others would say He simply fails to prevent tragedies from occurring. Pragmatically, though, the result is the same—we suffer, and whether God acts or doesn't act, He's still at the bottom of it. That means our true conflict is with God.

If we really want to start down the road of asking "why," let's not sell ourselves short of following it all the way to the end. At the end there's God. He's the one in control. He's the only being in the universe that is sovereign. He's the beginning and the end of all things, including our laments. And that's probably why we don't want to follow it all the way to the end because if God is at the end of that trail, then we aren't just asking why about the cancer. We are asking about the foundations of what we think—what we hope—is true. We are asking about the nature of good and evil. We are wondering about the validity of the love of God. We are pondering the extent of His compassion and wisdom. And in that kind of questioning, the basis of our whole existence is at stake. That's why we don't follow the trail all the way to the end—we're afraid of what we might find there. So we medicate, dripping spiritual and emotional morphine into ourselves so we don't have to face the ultimate reality of an uncomfortable conversation with an uncomfortable God.

That's a hard situation to be in for a nice, Christian boy like me. Sure, I had asked questions of God before, but they were raised in a sterile, academic environment. Those questions had the ring of queries like, "Could God make a rock so big He wasn't strong enough to move it?" or some such foolishness like it. But not now. These were questions from the waiting room. They were as regular as my two-year-old's need for morphine. But I took comfort that I wasn't the first one to ask such questions.

Job

The Bible is, among other things, an honest book. It's full of people who faced death, misery, and hardship of all kinds; and more times than not, the people in those stories came to the Lord to express their disappointment or confusion about their circumstances. I found myself gravitating toward the story of Job as an example of someone who refused to be medicated, though everyone in his life urged him to abandon his struggle for truth.

Job sensed something deeper was going on in the midst of his troubles, and he steadfastly pressed on into the midst of his pain. And there was a lot of pain.

Job was a rich man, an upstanding citizen of his community. He had a large family and wanted for nothing. And yet Job never took any of this for granted. He was continually on his knees before God, even going so far as regularly offering sacrifices on behalf of his children, just in case they had sinned. This was the pattern of Job's life, but unbeknownst to him, a cosmic conversation was going on with him at the center.

The faithfulness of Job was to be tested. Satan's charge against Job was that his life of allegiance was entirely contingent upon circumstance: "Of course Job is faithful to You. Look at what he has! But if his life started quaking at the foundations, if suddenly things weren't going so well for him, then he'd abandon his fidelity to You in a second." God took up the challenge on behalf of His man, and so the circumstances started to change. And they changed dramatically.

At God's permission, Satan systematically took apart Job's life, starting with his children. Then his property. Then his physical health. Job was eventually left poor, alone, and sick in emotional, physical, and spiritual pain. But why?

As readers, we know it was because of a bet, a cosmic wager with Job at the center. Job didn't have the luxury of reading about his story on the pages of a book, but he suspected there was something larger, some bigger purpose and reason, going on behind the scenes. So did we.

I remember pressing that morphine button over and over again. Pressing and wondering. Pressing and considering. Pressing and thinking. Was this a test of faith? Was there some heavenly conversation we weren't privy to happening at this moment? What was the bigger reason? Why was I standing over an IV pole rather than teaching my son the rules of tag and why Superman would whip Batman in a fight? Every time I started down that road of questioning, I pulled back. I stopped short. And that's the difference in Job's reaction and mine—he didn't look for a way to medicate his pain, a pill or a drip or a drink to numb his experience and provide a temporary means of escape. Instead, Job pressed hard into the pain, not running from it but engaging it. He was insistent in asking the hard questions of "how" and "why" about the tragedy that had become his life.

Not everybody in Job's life was content to do the same. In fact, much of the remaining biblical text is the record of his three friends who came to try and comfort him through the grieving process, but they had a slightly different take on what was happening than Job did.

These three guys were bent on the logic of the situation. They wanted to figure out what had happened, too, but they were absolutely unyielding in their black-and-white approach. They were insistent that what happened had to be Job's fault, that the circumstantial change was a result of some latent sin in his life. To their credit they were unwilling to call into question God's perfect justice, reasoning that in that justice Job needed to own up to his own fault. Job, on the other hand, was equally insistent that he was not to blame. He didn't know what was happening or why it was happening, but he knew the answer wasn't as simple as being punished for some sin he had committed.

Job was not content to settle for their logic; he had the sense that something deeper was going on in his life. And because he did, he did something that his three friends, with all their intelligent and reasoned approaches to faith never did throughout the book—he asked God about it. That's ultimately where Job's pressing-in led him—not to logic, or to reason, not to medication and not to therapy—it led him to the throne of the King of the universe:

"If only I had someone to hear my case! Here is my signature; let the Almighty answer me. Let my Opponent compose His indictment. I would surely carry it on my shoulder and wear it like a crown. I would give Him an account of all my steps; I would approach Him like a prince." (Job 31:35–37)

Job's engagement of his pain drove him to ask the real questions, the same questions anyone who has sat with pain inevitably comes to at the end:

"Why is this happening?"

"Is God real?"

"Can He hear me?"

"How can a loving God allow this to happen?"

Who

In Job 38 God started talking back. He answered Job out of a whirlwind, which must have been more than a little disconcerting. But after these thirty-seven chapters of accusations, questions, and pain, the answer God gave was not the "Why?" Job was looking for. It was the "Who" he wasn't.

For the next four chapters, God talked about . . . Himself. He talked about His power and His creativity. He talked about

His wisdom and His justice. And He reminded Job that he, as a human, possessed none of those qualities in comparison to the Almighty. Never once did God crack the door of eternity and say, "See, this whole thing started when Satan came walking in here. . . ." Never once did He take Job into the future to show him the good that would come from his struggle. Never once did He reveal the way He would redeem Job's pain. Never did God show Job one of the billions of Bibles that would be printed in the future, all containing his story. Not one single answer to Job's specific questions. Just descriptions of Himself.

While that may seem unsatisfying on our end, to know that God doesn't offer answers or promise a glimpse "on the inside," we've got to ask ourselves the question: Would knowing why really help? And at least for our part, the answer is no. It wouldn't. *Why* doesn't bring back the lost time. *Why* doesn't gather up the tears we've shed. *Why* doesn't make the ache go away. *Why* doesn't help with the anxiety of the future.

But "Who" does. God is the redeemer of moments small and large. God gathers up our tears and holds them in His hands. God is the healer of the soul. God is the caretaker of the future. *Who* helps tremendously in ways that *why* never could.

That's what Job's three friends were missing. It's incredibly ironic that in their attempt to protect God from Job's questions, they were actually trying to force their friend to settle for something less than the end of his questions. They were pushing him toward logic and reason, and while that has its place, in cases like this what we need isn't logic and reason. What the hurting person needs more than anything else is God.

Though I can't claim to know the enormity of Job's battle, I do know what it's like to be around well-intentioned but misguided people. Take the guy, for instance, who upon hearing the news about Joshua's diagnosis, gently and yet unmistakably implied that if Jana and I really believed strongly enough Joshua would be healed immediately. Or the other folks who seemed to come out of the woodwork with this cure or that one, berries or crystals or whatever. In each of these cases, we would just smile and say thank you for caring and then turn around and bad-mouth them behind their backs.

Probably shouldn't have done that.

At the same time we had a sense deep inside of us that we didn't need berries; we didn't need crystals; and in truth we didn't even really need answers, though we thought we did. What we really needed was God. We needed the *who* much more than the *why*.

When we are willing to push past the medication, to embrace the pain and the questions coming with it, we don't necessarily find all the answers—but we find God. He's at the core of our questions. And He Himself is the answer to our pain.

In the case of Joshua, I tried as best I could to do just that—to press in rather than escape. That pressing-in became a constant refrain of our time in and out of the hospital. Sometimes it felt frankly like there was nothing to press into, but then there were other times when we weren't rewarded with answers but with connection. And on the other end of that connection, we found that God was not emotionally distant from us but was in fact more than willing to cry alongside us. And those tears of the divine were more meaningful than any answers we might have received.

Chapter 4

Tears

Waiting

"Jesus loved Martha, her sister, and Lazarus. So when He heard that he was sick, He stayed two more days in the place where He was." (John 11:5–6)

About three months after Joshua was diagnosed with leukemia, I read those words from John 11. I had to squint to read them because the hospital room was dark. I had only the light coming from the bathroom to aid me.

We spent five of the first eight months sleeping on the sixth floor of Children's Hospital, in various amounts of time each trip. The most discouraging trip we had was the time we were released on a Saturday morning, went home, then returned that afternoon because Joshua got a fever. We actually came back to the same room. My pillow was still there, right where I mistakenly left it six hours earlier when we were discharged.

When a sick little boy goes to bed at 8:00 p.m., and the lights are off for the night in the hospital room, parents have to find ways to occupy their own minds. We certainly had plenty to think about—the constant phone conversations with insurance companies, the juggling of work responsibilities, and the studying of treatment protocols. In the darkness of those still, quiet moments, I thought a lot about faith and God, about suffering, and about how I felt about the whole thing. That's what brought me to this chapter of the Bible late that night, and I wasn't happy with what I found.

In John 11 I found a waiting Jesus. The problem with that, at least to me in that moment, was that "waiting" was about the furthest thing from what Jesus was supposed to be doing. I was convinced I knew what Jesus was supposed to do. He was supposed to be nice. He was supposed to care. To heal. To charge in and fix things. But not in this chapter. Here He was doing none of those things. He was just waiting.

Doubling my anxiety was the fact that I felt like He was doing the same thing in our case, which was nothing. Joshua didn't seem to be getting better; he seemed to be getting worse. It certainly wasn't from lack of prayer. We knew that scores of people all over the country and maybe even the world were praying for him. Scarcely was begging for the future of my son far from my own thoughts. So where was Jesus?

After all, God is supposed to *love* me.

There it was. God was supposed to love me. But my son had cancer. How do you square those two things with each other? Oh, I could run theological circles and make clever statements about how those things fit together, but still . . . late at night, with Joshua sleeping fitfully in his bed and me staring into the blackness in my chair with nothing but the bitterness and fear to keep me company, I knew that I had no answer. The bottom line was that if God loved me, He sure had a funny way of showing it.

"Loved"

A little boy with cancer is a situation I would try to keep from those I love. I'd guard them against it. I'd take precautions on their behalf. And if the worst should happen and I couldn't protect them, you better believe I'd be rushing to the hospital. Visiting. Caring. Providing. That's what I had done for Joshua. I'd done it because I loved him. But God? I couldn't say the same for Him. I prayed. I petitioned. I cried. And I felt . . . nothing. Emptiness. Despair. Isolation. Darkness.

Where was He, this God who so loved the world? Where was the great Healer? We needed Him there, in that cubicle of a hospital room. Doing something. Healing someone. Springing into action. I didn't need a Jesus that was sleeping in the boat while the storms raged around His friends. I needed a Jesus who was turning over the tables of sickness and disease and calling out cancerous cells like they were demons.

I felt a certain kinship with the sisters mentioned in John 11. Mary, Martha, and Lazarus weren't just any old people to Jesus. They weren't just faces in the crowd or casual bystanders to His ministry. Whenever Jesus traveled through the region of Bethany, He made time for this sister/sister/brother trio. He ate with them. He talked with them. He laughed with them. These people were like His family. So what did these people do when one of them got sick? They contacted Jesus. They knew Him well enough to know that a healing like this was small potatoes in His hands; they had seen Him do much more. And they knew how He felt about them. So when Lazarus became ill, the sisters sent word to Jesus, and their message didn't say, "Hey, Jesus, that guy you met that one time on a hillside somewhere, remember him? Well, he's sick." No, it was much more explicit than that: "Lord, the one you love is sick. The person you've sat around a table with and shared intimate moments with needs you."

Jesus got the message. The problem was what He did with it, or rather what He didn't do with it. What must it have been like for the sisters? I thought I knew. Surely it was similar to what I was experiencing that night. They must have sat by their brother's bed, too, watching him sweat out a fever. Seeing him squirm and moan in his sleep, wondering if they should call the doctor again. Every once in a while, getting up and walking to the window to see if someone was coming up the walk. Expecting, hoping, that maybe today would be the day Jesus would show up because in their hearts they knew that if He only would, then everything would change. Each day waking up wondering if the silence would end.

And then each night going to sleep wondering, *Where is our miracle?*

I thought He loved us.

I knew that just as I could relate to the sisters, Joshua, though he didn't know it, could relate to Lazarus, especially at night. The sores were still there on his mouth and his bottom. He would go to sleep only to moan in pain without waking up. Then, occasionally, he would release his bowels and wake up screaming in pain. I would change his diaper as quickly as I could and then sit with him in the rocking chair watching an episode of *Barney* until he fell back asleep. I'd repeated this process five or six times that particular night, and exhaustion was getting the better of me.

I found myself looking at the hospital door, maybe in much the same way Mary and Martha watched the door of their own house, expecting Jesus to come in at any moment.

He didn't. And Joshua continued to hurt. Meanwhile, I wondered if the minutes, hours, and eventually days of Joshua's life were ticking away, just as they had for Lazarus.

More Important

In my more reflective moments, when I wasn't watching the door for Jesus to barge into the room, I wondered the same thing Mary and Martha must have wondered: "What is keeping Him?" There had to be something, right? Something more vital. More precious. More imperative. But what?

Well, in the case of Lazarus, we actually know the answer. "This sickness . . . is for the glory of God, so that the Son of God may be glorified through it" (John 11:4). Jesus was delayed because the sickness was meant to glorify God.

That's funny, because you would think the opposite would be the case. It would make sense to me that it would be pretty God glorifying for our boy to be cured miraculously of cancer. We certainly would have jumped up and down. Heck, I would have shouted "Glory to God!" at the top of my lungs. So how did Jesus' inactivity serve to glorify God, in either the case of Lazarus or a two-year-old whose mouth and bottom wouldn't stop hurting? As soon as I asked the question, I knew the answer. I knew it from a logical standpoint, but I also knew it from an experiential standpoint. See, it's one thing for someone to say, "I just got bumped up to a six-figure income, bought a house in the burbs, and have a beautiful wife and 2.5 healthy children. Glory to God!" God should receive glory for all good things in our lives.

But it's an entirely different matter when people are weeping over the state of their circumstances, their health, and their world—yet they say along with Job in the Old Testament, "I know that my Redeemer lives" (Job 19:25 NASB). That's powerful. That is the evidence of someone who doesn't just stick with Jesus during the good times. That is the life that screams out to the world around it, "Jesus is enough. And He's better than all of these circumstantial and fleeting blessings." And that kind of person propels and magnifies the glory of God . . . even through their pain. They prove to a doubting world that Jesus is good enough to hang onto. Jesus understands better than we do that many times the most effective way for the glory of God to be advanced is through the suffering of His people.

Even three months into our journey with cancer, I saw the same dynamic happening. The Lord was using Joshua and our family to encourage others in similar circumstances. He was drawing people that loved this little boy to a deeper dependence on Him and moving them into more and more activity in prayer. From the beginning we tried to be open and honest about our fears, hopes, doubts, and confidences. And we tried to hang onto faith.

People told us that the shreds of our faith were moving them to trust God more, and so we saw that God was already bringing good out of our tough situation. So I got it. I still get it—pain is the avenue through which the glory of God can advance, both in ancient Palestine and in Vanderbilt Children's Hospital.

Furthermore, I recognized (at least intellectually) the importance of the glory of God. It's obviously important to Jesus. That was the impetus for His inactivity. The only reasonable conclusion we can draw is that the glory of God is more important. It's more important than the sisters' emotional turmoil. It's more important than Lazarus. It's more important than you, and it's more important than me. And the uncomfortable realization in that hospital room was that it was more important than my little boy. But you'll forgive me if I didn't screw on a smile and say, "Of course! I should have known. It all makes sense now. By all means, Jesus, take your time."

Even if we can accept Jesus' reason for waiting, we still have to deal with the consequences.

Consequences

There are consequences when Jesus does nothing. God may eventually be glorified in every situation, but my son battled cancer and the pain of ongoing chemotherapy side effects while Jesus waited. My wife and I battled depression and overwhelming anxiety while Jesus waited. And in the story, when at last Jesus made His way to Bethany, Lazarus was dead and had been in the tomb for four days.

Four days is a significant detail in this story because it left no doubt about the fate of Lazarus. We might wonder why it would take four days to remove hope from the situation, but remember that medical technology in the first century was obviously not what it is today. It was not extremely uncommon for people to be pronounced dead only to wake up from some kind of comatose state. In fact, after someone was assumed to be dead, people would examine the body, even going out to the cemetery to do so, up to three days after death, just to make sure.

Additionally, Jewish folklore held that at death the soul would return to the body for up to four days, each time checking to see if the physical body could receive it back. After the fourth day the body would have begun to decompose, and the soul would move on. Put those things together and you get what the Bible means when it says "four days"—it means there was no hope left in Bethany. Lazarus was gone. He was undeniably dead.

While we can say that casually, Mary and Martha could not. I wondered in the darkness what those four days were like for them, having called out to their dear friend Jesus and received the cold shoulder. Maybe they held onto hope to the last moment; maybe even past the last moment. But no more. They had moved past any shred of optimism they were clinging to and into their grief. And they were definitely grieving.

When Jesus waited, He not only ensured a certain death for Lazarus, but He ensured that Mary and Martha would have begun sitting shi'vah, the prescribed seven-day grieving process for Jewish persons who lost someone in their immediate family. It's still practiced among Jewish folks today, and it dates all the way back to Job's friends who sat with him for seven days to comfort him. The mourner sits shoeless on the floor or a low stool in the home of the dead. They don't work; they don't play. They don't even have to go to synagogue. They just sit. And no one can talk to them. The community just sits together with them in their grief.

I wonder if God knew a long time ago that religious people have the propensity to say the stupidest things in moments of tragedy:

"He's in heaven now, sweetie."

"There's a reason for everything."

"God works all things for the good."

It's as if someone else's pain makes us so uncomfortable that we automatically try to stop it from happening. Those things are true; they're just inappropriate. But not in the house of someone sitting shi'vah. There's silence there. People can deal with pain there. That's what the sisters were doing. And in their pain, they knew they were grieving because Jesus waited.

While the sisters were grieving, I was getting angry. Furious.

Finally

It wasn't that I didn't want God to be glorified. It was that I resented my son is being used for such a cause, as good a cause as it is. A question welled up inside of me. Maybe you know how it feels to have a question like that; it nags at you especially during times of suffering. Many times the question is so difficult that it's pushed aside by those who want so badly to honor God with their lives. But every once in a while the question becomes too much, and so it must be voiced. No matter how committed we are to that which is truly valuable, we can't help but ask, "What about my brother?" or "What about my mom?" or "What about my life?" or "What about my son?" We know the glory of God is important, but what about the casualties left in the wake?

Of course, we rarely ask those questions. We eat them away. Or drink them away. Or smoke them away. Or "church" them away. Anything but ask them, because spiritual people don't have questions. They just believe, . . . right? But that wasn't enough for me. Not that night. And not for Mary either, I think.

Jesus did eventually show up, and Mary was ready for Him. Martha was a little more ready to accept what had happened. She met Jesus outside of town, and Jesus answered her with a message about resurrection and life that has become the ground of hope for a multitude of believers who have lost loved ones. But as He went into Bethany, He found another sister that wanted something more.

Mary was different from Martha. There is another account in Scripture of Jesus' interactions with this family, and it reveals the starkly different personalities of the sisters. Luke 10 records the story of a time when Jesus was staying at their house. Martha was busy while Jesus taught—straightening, cooking, cleaning, preparing. It's no wonder she was ready to get out of the house and run to meet Jesus—she was a doer by nature. But Mary was different. She spent the day that seemed like a distant memory sitting at Jesus' feet as He taught. She listened. She considered. She reflected.

Mary was a thinker. And over the week of her brother's death, she had plenty of time to think and plenty to think about. I'm sure she battled with her thoughts, trying to think and believe the right thing. Her internal dialogue may have gone something like this: *I know Jesus has a reason. I know He loves us. But I also know that He could have healed my brother. So there must have been a good reason He didn't come. But what about Lazarus? What could be so important to keep Jesus from being here?* Mary had plenty of time to try and piece things together, but in the end, no matter how much she tried to comfort herself with all the right "church" answers, the question was too much.

Haven't we all had that experience? It's the moment when all the things we have read in the Bible collide full force with the circumstances of pain in our lives. We know that God ultimately acts in our best interests. We know that He has a plan. We believe He is in control. Yet we also know the pain of loss, grief, and disappointment. And for thinkers like Mary, a moment comes when theology fails and that nagging question bubbles to the surface.

So when Martha returned to tell Mary that Jesus had indeed finally come and was asking for her, she agreed to come out. *Come out?* she must have thought. *You're darn right I'll come out. I need answers.* And so she went—immediately. She raised herself up, fighting back tears of anger, and walked out the front door with such resolve that a crowd followed her there. She walked into the sunlight to see the face of Jesus across the dirt yard. She paused at the sight of Him but then regained her composure and walked until she was nose to nose with the One she thought was their friend.

Mary had thought about her question for days, and now it was time to ask. She wanted to put her finger in His face and say all the things in her heart. Then all her boldness and bravery suddenly collapsed, and she fell at His feet in a heap of tears. Through desperate sobs Mary looked up and finally gave voice to her doubts and fears: "Why did You not come? If You had been here, my brother would not have died. . . . What about my brother?"

That moment of being nose to nose with Jesus came for me well past midnight that night in the rocking chair in the hospital. Joshua had waked up and gone back to sleep ten times that night under the aid of his morphine drip, temporarily relieved of pain. But at that moment he had been awakened with a dirty diaper, the sores on his bottom flaring up in pain. And he wouldn't go back to sleep. I tried to get him to watch a video. Nothing. I tried to get him to drink some juice, but the sores on his mouth hurt too badly. I resorted to holding him in my arms tightly, rocking back and forth, back and forth, humming a song. And he slept in ten-minute increments for the rest of the night.

I, meanwhile, found myself looking up at the ceiling saying things to God I ought not have said. Pouring out my anger and frustration at His inactivity, figuratively waving my finger in His face. My claim was simple: "I get that this is all, in some way, for the glory of God. And I'm a big supporter of that. But what about my son?"

Rage

Good Christians like me know that the glory of God is important and even that God's glory is seen through our circumstances, painful though they may be. We also want to embrace the glory for the sake of what is most important, but we understand Mary's question too. It surfaces when the fact that all things work together for good just doesn't seem to be enough (Rom. 8:28). It comes to the forefront when you grapple with reality even if you know theologically that in some mysterious way God will be glorified through bad times. This cancer is somehow for God's glory. This car accident is somehow for God's glory. This job loss is somehow for God's glory. But it doesn't make sense in the moment. In the moment all you know is that your little boy is in pain. And so are you. That's when we ask the question.

What about my brother? What about my mom? What about my friend? What about my life?

So how does Jesus handle that finger in His face? And how does He interact with a woman weeping in the dust? As Mary collapsed at Jesus' feet, the text says "He was angry in His spirit and deeply moved" (John 11:33). Isn't that nice. Deeply moved in spirit and troubled. I'll admit it—I'd rather have some miraculous healing action springing from His fingertips than a "moved" Jesus. But something else is present in that phrase.

Other translations of that verse use stronger wording. Many record that sadness was not the only emotion Jesus felt; they indicate that He felt anger—and not just any anger. "Angry in His spirit and deeply moved" carries a sense of especially strong anger, even indignation and rage. Why was Jesus angry?

Maybe He was mad at Mary. Who was she, after all, to question what He did or did not do? Didn't she understand that He had a mission, and that meant hard decisions? In fact, wasn't she calling into question the value of the kingdom of God? Besides, in about five minutes He was going to turn the funeral into a party—but there she was, crying on the ground. Pathetic. And maybe He was enraged at me, too, rocking in that chair as if the future of redemptive history depended on whether or not my son could sleep. Surely He would have the right to be a little annoyed at my indignation.

Dusty Tears

But I don't buy that. I don't think Jesus was mad at the grieving sister, mainly because He wasn't just angry—He was also moved. Deeply. Profoundly. Maybe Jesus was angry not because Mary was sad but because she *had* to be sad.

Jesus understands better than we do that many times the most effective way for the glory of God to be advanced is through the suffering of His people. He is the God of the cross, the one who endured great suffering Himself for the glory of God. So He, more than anyone else, understands that suffering is an incredibly powerful avenue for God's glory to go out. He knows it, but He doesn't have to like it. I think that's why He was angry. And I think that's why, as we see in verse 35, He wept.

In His tears you can almost hear His explanation: "I am so sorry that it has to be this way."

Is it possible that Jesus' rage is directed at the fact that the world is so broken, so sinful, so far away from faith and the gospel, that the only way to get through the message of hope the cross offers is through the suffering of God's children? Is it possible that Jesus saw the aftermath of that suffering and was angry that this is the way it has to be? Angry at the effects of sin? Angry at the pain of His children? Jesus looked, He took in the situation, and He wept. Amazing.

Can you fathom that? The God of the universe cried. Thinking about it is heart stopping. And it sort of makes you ask what the bigger miracle of this passage is—is it a Jesus who can raise the dead, or a Jesus who weeps alongside His friends even though He knows He's going to do so?

Jesus' tears are meaningful. But the other thing that was meaningful to me was what Jesus didn't say. He makes no effort to justify Himself. He doesn't bother to give Mary a lesson on the importance of sacrifice for the sake of God. He doesn't launch into a theological treatise about what is really important in the universe. And He doesn't make some pithy statement about how everything will be OK in heaven someday. He simply weeps. Sometimes the tears are better than the explanation.

Immanuel

In the chair that night, I didn't get a miracle, or at least not the kind I thought I needed. And I didn't get a big explanation of what was going on. I certainly didn't get a message from God telling me just to suck it up and remember the cause of the glory of God. But I did get something—tears. Both mine and His.

That's the kind of Jesus we follow. He is not one who simply barks orders onto the battlefield of life, telling us to go here or there, do this or that. We do not follow an ivory-tower Jesus.

The Christ we follow knows the full range of human experience. He is not an isolated God but one intimately acquainted with the pain of the human condition. He is Immanuel, God with us. We may rest assured that whatever situation we find ourselves in, God is emotionally involved there too. When we weep at the death of a loved one, our Jesus weeps as well. When we rejoice because all is well, His shouts of joy eclipse our own. And when we fall in the dirt before Him—so sure of theological facts yet emotionally destroyed by the circumstances of this sinful world—He falls down and weeps with us.

This is our God. This is the God who knew the end before the beginning. He is the One who knew the resurrection before the crucifixion. He is the One who knew the glory before the pain. Because He knows those things, He can make grand promises about the eternal glory that awaits all those who are His. Yet His response to us in the pain of the human condition is not, "Just believe! It will all be over soon. This is nothing compared to what awaits you." Instead, His response is to walk through the pain with us. His response is to offer His abiding presence in the form of the Holy Spirit until the day God receives the glory He deserves.

At the end of this life He will still be there with us, but we will be seated together beside the throne of the Father, scarcely able to remember those times when He knelt in the dirt beside us and wept.

But until that time maybe sometimes what we need more than just another explanation, another cliché, or another promise of heaven . . . is tears. Tears of the One who understands. Tears of the One who empathizes. Tears of the One who doesn't just tell us that everything will be OK in the end but of the One who feels our pain as deeply as we do.

Chapter 5

Identity

―――――

Money

It didn't take long for me to figure out a few things about having a kid with cancer. I knew right away, for example, that it was going to be imperative for me to learn how to describe succinctly what was happening in our lives. Every person I saw wanted to know how Joshua was doing. And though their intentions were always good and noble, most weren't wanting to get into a two-hour conversation about it. They wanted a quick update, so I learned how to boil down his treatment, reactions, prognosis, and mental state to about three sentences.

I also learned this—chemotherapy is expensive. Not expensive like, "Man, can you believe it costs ten dollars to go to the movies?" But expensive like, "This could throw our family into financial ruin." After the first month of living in the hospital, I got an itemized bill for everything, and the number at the bottom made me throw up in my mouth a little bit. Between medicines, in-room therapy, grilled-cheese sandwiches, diapers, X-rays, scans, and everything else, the only other time I'd seen a number like that was when I signed up for a mortgage. That's not to mention the other costs associated with prolonged stays in the hospital.

Most meals had to be eaten out rather than cooked. It was a forty-five minute trip to and from the hospital, and I could almost hear the gas guzzling out of the tank as we went back and forth to do laundry, get a new stuffed animal, or mow the yard. And numerous prescriptions had to be filled on what seemed to be a daily basis. At some point, faced with costs like that, you just resign yourself to the spending and fork over the plastic over and over again.

I was trying to lead our family through this time, and part of that meant keeping an eye on the consistently dwindling balances. We were getting poorer by the day. Sometimes by the hour.

But blessed are the poor, right? Jesus said that. Here was yet another verse from the Bible I had been able to keep at an arm's length up to that point in life. But suddenly we weren't just talking about being poor; we were heading that direction.

And I felt far from blessed. Blessed would mean not having to check my balance every day. It would mean not having to transfer money in and out of accounts to make sure we weren't overdrawn.

That's not to say I was confused about why the poor are blessed. I thought I knew, at least intellectually. It is because when you are poor, you have much less of a chance to be lured away from faith by money and the things it can buy. The poor don't have the luxury of putting their faith in financial security or buying up pleasures of this world. They are prime candidates to fully believe and embrace the gospel because there is not much standing in the way. They simply have no other source of hope.

Because I knew these things, I had always been able to look down my nose at someone like the rich, young ruler. In the book of Matthew, this man is called young. Luke makes clear that he was a ruler of some kind. And both point to the fact that he had great wealth. That's why we call him "The Rich, Young Ruler." The Bible tells us that crowds were following Jesus wherever He went in those days, and there must have been a sharp contrast between this guy and the crowd pressing in on Him. They were dirty; he was clean. They were poor; he was rich. They were shabby; he was finely dressed. He had a simple and straightforward question for Jesus: "What do I need to do to inherit eternal life?"

Jesus responded that he should keep the law. The man claimed that he was already doing that. Wasn't there something more? And that's when Jesus came with the zinger—"Sell it all. Become poor. Then you can follow Me." The Bible says that the man went away sad because he had great wealth.

Clearly he didn't get how blessed it was to be poor. For the first time, making those almost hour-long trips to and from the hospital, I identified with this young man rather than scorned him. What would I have done in the same position? I'd like to think I would have sold everything. But given how "unblessed" I felt during those days, I wasn't so sure.

But the truth was, as much as I worried about our money, something else bothered me. I was becoming poor in other ways, too.

Despite the enormity of those costs, we had one thing on our side—insurance. We were covered, and though I got the whole bill for each trip to the ER and each hospital stay, I was only responsible for a small portion of those many visits. I could handle that.

And so began my ongoing conversations with insurance companies, hospital administrators, and billing offices, trying to negotiate coverages and noncoverages, in-patient and out-patient, referrals and everything else. But at the end of the day, regardless of the headaches associated with the bureaucratic process, insurance would keep us afloat financially. Insurance was essential for our future stability. But that presented a problem.

When Joshua was diagnosed, our insurance came through Jana's job of teaching fourth grade at Winstead Elementary School. She was doing that because I was trying to make it as an independent contractor of sorts. For as long as I can remember, I've wanted to be my own boss and for my job to be that of a writer and a speaker at churches, conferences, and events. That's what I was doing. I even had a Web site (though it was far from awesome). As such, my job mainly consisted of being a stay-at-home dad, working while Joshua was in child care, when he took naps, early in the morning and late at night. And because most conferences I spoke at happened over the weekend, I frequently traveled. But when the diagnosis came down, we knew something had to change.

I wasn't making enough money yet to solely support our family. And I certainly didn't have the patience to be the primary caregiver for a little boy who was going to need round-the-clock attention. That, combined with the fact that both Jana and I knew that emotionally she needed to be the one staying with Joshua, led me to conclude that a drastic career change was in order. If I could get a regular job, one with health benefits, then Jana could stay with Joshua. We would make it. And even in this need, the Lord had been thinking ahead.

I had done some writing for an organization in Nashville called Lifeway Christian Resources and through that process had made some good friends. The day Joshua was diagnosed, I sent out a massive e-mail to everyone I knew asking them to pray for us, and a few people from that organization were on the list. Two hours after we learned our son had leukemia, when we were sitting in a hospital room, I looked out the window to see a man whose first name I thought was Jim. Somehow he had snuck past the nurses on guard duty and had made it all the way into the sequestered hallway of the sixth floor, and there he was at my door.

Jim was one of the friends I'd made, though I'd only called him Mr. Johnston up to that point. He was the guy who had gotten me my check for the work I'd done. As I walked into the hallway, Jim hugged me, pressed $100 dollars into my hand, and asked me if I needed a job.

Two months later I went shopping for five new pairs of khaki pants, some button-down shirts, took a drug test, and started work as an editor. Never had I been so convinced that this was the way God had provided for our family. Never had I been more thankful to be sitting in an office with my shirt tucked in. Never had I marveled more at God's grace. And at the same time, never had I felt more guilty because of the intense conflict I felt inside.

Good-bye, Dreams

Sometimes you just do what you have to do, no questions asked. And in that moment I would have taken a job as a fry cook, international spy, real estate agent, or garbage man. Whatever. It was simply and amazingly the grace of God that He handed me a job where I had my hand in producing Bible studies that churches use around the world. Given that, you would think a guy would be overwhelmed with gratitude, right? That's what I thought, too, and that's why I felt so guilty.

On the one hand I was overwhelmed. It was amazing. I was thankful. But on the other hand this new life was a radical departure from what I assumed my life would be like. I had figured that God's big idea for me was to be a communicator, through both writing and teaching. But I found myself working as an editor, forming and fashioning someone else's words. I wasn't a writer, not a real one anyway. These weren't my thoughts and ideas. And that was really, hard.

We often think about the grieving process exclusively in terms of people. You lose someone close to you, and you lament that loss in personal and profound ways. But the same process happens, I believe, to other areas of life, too—like the moment you realize you're never going to be a doctor. When you first know that you can't have children naturally. When you realize you may never meet the right person and get married. You grieve what your life was "supposed" to be as you try to adjust to how your life is. You have a great sense of loss and sorrow, and that sense of loss can be compounded by guilt because you know you have plenty to be thankful for.

Dreams can be grieved over much the same way people can, especially if that dream is the source of your self-definition. In the end grieving is about loss and finding your way through life without that thing that's not there anymore.

That's what I tried to do. With Joshua still in the hospital a lot, I settled into the ritual of ironing pants on a small countertop next to a bedpan and extra diapers. Our schedule looked like this: Jana was pregnant with our second child so we decided she had no business sleeping in a hospital room; I did most of that. I would turn off the lights with Joshua at eight, sit in the dark for a couple of hours, eventually fall asleep, and wake up at 7:00. Jana arrived around 8:00. I'd take a shower and go to work until 5:00. We'd have dinner together; then Jana would leave the hospital for our house across town at about 7:30. Then we'd wake up and do it all over again. Most days I spent at least the first hour of the day after I got to my office thinking about what our lives had become.

I would trudge into the building, sometimes feeling that it took a sustained effort to budge my hand from my side to push the button on the elevator. With great effort I'd walk to my office, and more than once a week, I'd shut the door. And just sit there. On worse days I would lie down and cry into the stain-resistant carpet. Cry for Joshua. For Jana. For our lives. For my dreams. For what life was supposed to be like.

Poor

The question of identity bothered me the most. In my most honest moments, I had to admit that I didn't have any idea who I was anymore. Six months before, I knew exactly who I was— preacher, writer, networker, mover, and shaker (at least in my own mind). I was the guy who flew in on an airplane, stayed in a hotel room, and wore jeans with carefully (and expensively) crafted holes in the knees. But now? Now I wore khakis. I sat behind a computer. I spent hours on the phone with insurance companies and then sorted through corporate policies at my new job. And though I harbored an incredible amount of guilt for feeling the way I did, I missed my old life. Everything that had made me feel important and significant was gone, and I was facing a crisis of self-identification.

I felt poor, not just in the wallet but in my sense of self.

Poor is more than a description of a financial state. It's a state of being. And according to Jesus, being poor is being blessed. That's where He was taking the rich young ruler—to the blessing of poverty. And that's also where it felt like I was headed, minus the blessing part.

Before Joshua was diagnosed, I felt like I was rich with dreams. And if I'm completely honest, many of those dreams centered around me—what I might accomplish, where I might go, what I might do. But with the onset of leukemia and everything associated with it, I felt those dreams being tugged away from me one by one. I wasn't going to be the preacher people lined up to hear. I wasn't going to be a great person of influence. I wasn't going to be a famous author. I was going to be . . . normal. And that scared the life out of me. The resulting feeling was one of poverty, of feeling like there was little left to hold onto for the future. In that poverty I lacked real self-definition.

For a long time I had enjoyed introducing myself to people. After names are exchanged, the next question in most circles centers around occupation, and I liked the nifty list of accomplishments and projects I was involved in that I could recite at a moment's notice when the question came up: "Well, I'm a writer and speaker. Yes, I've had some things published, and I'm working on a few projects right now. And yes, as a matter of fact, you can make a living as a communicator. I'm flying to this place next week, then the next week I've got an event here . . ." Blah, blah, blah.

When I started working at my new job, those introductions were incredibly difficult for me to make: "My name is Michael. I'm an editor." In fact, for at least a year, I felt it necessary to qualify the description of my job: "I'm an editor, but I also have done some writing, and I still occasionally travel to preach at certain places." I was holding onto those remnants of my pre-leukemia life because without them I had no idea who I was. I needed them because I couldn't deal with the poverty of not having them.

My hunch is that this is what happens to most everyone who encounters an event like cancer and then tries to figure out what life looks like afterward. Such circumstances are painful for a lot of reasons, but one of the primary ones is because they are stripping—they strip us of money, power, prestige, health, or a loved one. And they change our lives, forcing us to ask the difficult questions of personal identity. Who are you now that you're not rich anymore? Who are you now that you don't work at your former job anymore? Who are you now that you can't exercise like you used to because of your illness? Who are you now that you have lost someone close to you? Who are you? And who am I? Pain strips us of the comfortable self-designations that we so desperately cling to. Pain makes us poor. I was impoverished in my identity. And maybe, whether he recognized it or not, that was part of the reason the rich, young ruler walked away from Jesus that day, too.

It's fairly telling that we even call him the rich, young ruler. We have no idea what his name was. All we know about him boils down to these three facts: Rich. Young. Ruler. That's his identity, recorded for all posterity. So when Jesus asked him to sell all his possessions, He was forcing that wealthy young man to give up his marks of self. Without those things he would be nobody. No one would even know what to call him. But in selling off those marks of identity, he would be positioning himself to truly become a follower of Jesus, for true Christians are by necessity poor.

A little detail in the account of the rich, young ruler helps bring the true purposes of Jesus into sharp focus. In Mark 10:21, we find Jesus' command to the young man: "Then, looking at him, Jesus loved him and said to him, 'You lack one thing: Go, sell all you have and give it to the poor, and you will have treasure in heaven. Then come, follow Me.'" Jesus looked at the man and loved him. He loved him in his wealth. He loved him before he asked him to do anything. Jesus loved the man before he refused the command to do more.

The legalist in me wants to reverse the order. I've often lived like the passage says that Jesus told him to go sell everything he owned; and then, after he hypothetically did it, Jesus looked at him and loved him. When we put love at the end rather than the beginning, we wind up bitter and frustrated over what we have to give up in our pursuit of Christ. We live a jaded existence in an endless effort to prove ourselves to God, trying to earn His approval with each act of goodness. But since the command comes after the love, regardless of what the command is, the only option for us is to believe that the command of Christ is made *out* of that love. Not to garner it.

In love Jesus was forcing this man to the point where he had nothing left to define himself. Then, with nothing to offer and with open hands, he could truly approach Jesus and know what Christianity was all about.

In the case of the rich, young ruler, Jesus invited him to such a state. He was doing the same thing with me, though our circumstances were different. Pain forces us to question the source of our self-worth. Becoming poor greatly aided me in rediscovering the fullness of the gospel that we often sell short.

Trees

There, sitting in my office, forcibly impoverished in spirit, I found myself looking at the gospel and Christianity not so much as an expression of what I do but as the definition of myself.

Jesus alludes to this idea, among other places, in Matthew 12. Jesus had been facing off against a group of religious teachers who charged Him with everything from being possessed by a demon to blasphemy. Finally fed up with the disparaging remarks of the Pharisees, Jesus spins on His heels and counters: "Pharisees, would you like to know what your real problem is? Some might say it's that you lie. Or that you steal. Or that you lust or tie heavy burdens on men's backs. Those are all symptoms. And you can try to clean up your behavior if you want to, but that doesn't solve the problem. The problem is that you're the wrong kind of tree."

Jesus goes on to develop the tree thing like this: "If you have an orange tree in your backyard, but you like apples, the solution to the problem isn't to just try and rip all the oranges off the tree. They'll come back. Neither is the solution to go and pick some apples and staple them to the branches of the tree. The solution is to dig up the old tree, throw it away, and plant a new one in its place."

The Pharisees might well have been able to will themselves to stop cheating. And lying. And stealing. But ultimately, those are all temporary Band-Aids that wouldn't address the real, underlying, deep issue. The real issue was (and remains) the heart. And the Pharisees had the wrong kind.

This is what being born again is all about—the Holy Spirit coming with the cosmic backhoe, digging up the tree of your heart and planting a new one in its place. The Bible is pretty clear that there are only two kinds of people in the world: those who live in darkness and those who live in light, those who have fellowship with God and those who don't, those who love the world and those who love God. Scripture is filled with contrasts: night and day, death and life, dark and light, lost and found. There is no middle ground. This mysterious love of God moves men and women from one category to the other. Salvation and life with Jesus lead to a core change in who you are—a complete redefinition of your identity. That's why Jesus' command to the rich, young ruler was out of love. Jesus wanted to strip this man from all the things in his life that defined him so that he could be redefined as Jesus wanted.

The man knew how people defined him. People defined him the same way we define him today—as rich, as young, and as a ruler. Jesus wanted more for him. He wanted to get to this man's core, to his real self. Selling his possessions would strip this man of his marks of identity. Only by stripping those things away, in that moment of crisis, could he define himself the way Jesus wanted—by his faith.

But the question of identity can really only be answered in a moment of crisis. In other words, it can only be answered when something attached to our core is taken out of our control: health, achievements, career, family life, and so forth. Who are you when those things are altered or threatened? Who would the rich, young ruler be if he sold his possessions? He would not be rich or a ruler; he would have nothing external left to define himself. He would be poor. A nobody. That poverty opens the door for Jesus to say, "Let me tell you who you really are."

Siblings and Children

So who are we? When we are stripped of those marks of self-identification we hold so dear and left confused and dejected about our identities, what does Jesus say? When we, either willingly or unwillingly, sell our marks of self-identification and become nobodies, how does He respond? Jesus redefines us as something else. He might define us as forgiven people. He might define us as accepted people. But He actually goes further than that. We have been moved, as Christians, well beyond being "just" forgiven and accepted. We've been moved all the way to children. We have been moved to adoption, and this adoption is important for us to understand and embrace.

In Jesus' day adoption was at the same time an entrance and an exit. A child was brought into a new family relationship where he now had new privileges and responsibilities as a member of the family. But at the same time there was a complete and total break from all previous rights and duties of his former family. In a Roman context a father could extend the privilege of adoption based on his pleasure and affection, and the new relationship was absolutely and severely binding. It was, indeed, a change of kingdoms. Because of the power structure of the Roman family, the adopted child was absolutely bound, as a slave was bound, to his new family. That kid was transferred from the power of his natural father to the power of his new one. And there was a price to be paid. The child was "bought," in a sense. This is what God has done for us. He has not only brought us out of one environment of sin and death; He has brought us into a new environment, one in which Jesus Christ is our brother as well as the ransom paid. And we are coheirs of the kingdom of God. It's staggering—we are children of God.

As you scan through the pages of Scripture, we find that God is concerned that we know we are adopted. In fact, this is one of the continual jobs of the Holy Spirit. In Romans 8, as well as Galatians 4, Paul reminds us that the Holy Spirit testifies and reminds us we are the children of God. The Holy Spirit causes us to cry out to our Abba—our Daddy—reminding us again we are His children. Fundamentally, we are children of God. We are the brothers and sisters of Jesus. And we remain so regardless of what happens in our lives. Regardless of our occupation, our financial state, or our health. We are children of God. Poverty opens the door for us to realize it fully.

Most of us live our entire lives without even beginning to grasp the immensity of what God has done for us in Christ. We pile job titles, degrees, and accolades on ourselves; and, even if we are Christians, we begin to define ourselves by those things. But when we suddenly become poor—well, poverty opens the door for Jesus to remind us who we really are in Him.

Slowly, with much reminding from the Holy Spirit, I began to see my worth and identity not defined by whether I wore jeans or khakis. Not whether I wrote books. Not whether I sat in an office or traveled on an airplane. I began slowly to embrace the fact that leukemia had stripped me of my former identity, but Jesus had stepped in to remind me that at my core, regardless of anything else, I am and will always be His brother. Armed with that knowledge, I can better face the challenges of this life, the tears of loss, and the inevitable circumstances that will again and again take me back to the base level of poverty.

And at the base level I will find Jesus still loving me, reminding me once again that I'm defined by Him and not by my external circumstances. By the grace of God that strips me of self-definition, I'll be able to stand and introduce myself like this: "My name is Michael. I'm a brother of Jesus. I'm a child of God."

Chapter 6

Between

Steroids

I walked into the hospital room after having gone for a run. Exercise was important for both Jana and me during those days, a great time to decompress and release stress. I walked in, sweating a lot, and found Joshua sitting in his bed behind a bowl of mac and cheese. That was a familiar sight, thanks to the steroids.

Contrary to popular belief, steroids don't always make you grow big and strong, although I did see an after-school special starring Ben Affleck where he pitched a pretty mean road-rage fit. I remembered Ben's outburst as we settled into the broader scope of Joshua's treatment because Joshua had to take steroids. A lot of them.

Because chemotherapy isn't smart enough to separate the cancer cells from other cells, the cells that protected our little boy and helped him fight off things like colds and flus and strep throat were dying along with the rogue blood cells. This constant barrage on his system left him defenseless against disease and generally worn out. No energy. No defense system. Enter steroids.

He was prescribed steroids to take simultaneously with the chemotherapy to counteract the negative effects of the chemo and overall keep him healthier. Seems logical to me. Unfortunately, the steroids came with their own set of side effects. While most folks are familiar with the side effects of chemotherapy—hair loss, nausea, and lethargy among others—the steroid effects are less publicized. Far from immediately being able to hit ninety-five home runs in a baseball season, Joshua suffered from two main things as a result of his roids: hunger and mood swings.

It's difficult to pen the amount of food I've seen my son put down because it sounds unbelievable when you read it. Trust me, it's true. I have the bank statements to prove it. Whether he was really hungry or he just needed something in his mouth at all times, his appetite became insatiable. Three breakfasts, two lunches, two afternoon snacks, large dinner, and then bedtime snack usually covered it. For some reason black olives and crackers that looked like airplanes you can only get on

Southwest Airlines flights were what he craved most in those days.

As tough as the constant questions and desire for more food were to deal with, tougher still were the emotional effects from his medicine. Dexamethesone, Joshua's particular brand of steroid, is a mood-altering drug. And moody he was, both ways. I've never seen him be more affectionate than when he is on steroids, climbing into your lap and kissing you all over your face, always wanting to be held close and cuddled. Then, like Bruce Banner getting angry, he would suddenly turn green and rip his shirt off when the smallest thing didn't go his way, collapsing into tears on the floor. It was heartbreaking to watch.

The physical and emotional effects were visible to everyone. Joshua stopped walking much because the chemo made his legs hurt. On those few days we actually got to spend at home, I would carry him down the stairs so he didn't have the pain in his joints of bending them at the knee in order to traverse our two-story house. Midday, I'd carry him back up the stairs so he could take a fitful hour-long nap. Then I'd carry him back down after it was done. And as I gathered him up in my arms those several times a day, I noticed that he was becoming heavier. Or squishier, to put it more accurately. He started to retain water, and eventually his clothes became too small for his bulging belly. I have vivid memories of him pushing around on his newly formed double chin, as if he knew something didn't feel right on his face. He hobbled and waddled around the hospital and eventually the house as best he could, but it was obvious that he was simply and completely uncomfortable. Uncomfortable with the hunger, uncomfortable with the pain, uncomfortable with his clothes—uncomfortable in every way.

The treatment protocol was intense, especially starting out. Joshua received weekly, if not daily, injections of chemotherapy through a port implanted in his chest. He also received chemotherapy directly into his spinal fluid via a spinal tap, all of which made him feel pretty crummy. That's how it was for about eighteen weeks, and for the first three months, he was on the steroids, too. Only a few days before I walked into the room after the run, I sat at our dining room table having a conversation with a friend. Joshua was just lying on the couch. It was like he couldn't lie still, and every ten seconds he would grunt and move, trying with all his might to get comfortable. And in a very honest and vulnerable moment, I confessed to my friend that I wondered if I would ever again see the little boy I thought I knew again. Because this didn't seem like him. So tired. So large. So uncomfortable. None of his toys held interest any more, and all he wanted to do was eat and watch videos.

Suffice it to say, I wasn't surprised to find him eating that day. At most times during the day, he was slurping down applesauce. Or eating crackers. Or dry cereal. Or wet cereal. Anything to keep his belly (and his mind) occupied during the midst of those painful days. You would put down a bowl or a plate of something, turn around, and it would be gone. Quick as lightning. And for months we had the difficult task of having to tell our son, "Enough." He would cry when we did. Say his stomach hurt. Or his legs. And that just another cup of peaches would make it feel better.

Something was different about his eating that particular day though. Each time he would put his spoon in his mouth, he would start to chew and then drop his spoon. He would make a funny face, then stick out his tongue, and brush at it with both his hands as if trying to clear something away. I saw that Jana was watching him go through this ritual with great interest, and I sat beside her. We watched him a while longer, trying to decide what he was doing. Then all at once it hit us: his hair.

Hair

Joshua always had great hair. We liked to keep it long, mainly because it looked so darn cool. It was rarely combed and would fall across his face in the way that people pay hundreds of dollars to achieve. Now his beautiful, golden, rock-star-quality hair was falling out into his macaroni.

We had held onto hope up until that point that maybe Joshua would be the one in fifty cancer kids who didn't have the side effect of complete hair loss. That maybe, just maybe, he would not have the classic branding of the telethons, alerting everyone in his path something was wrong. But it was happening. Joshua, my sweet little two-year-old son, was losing his hair. And it potentially would never come back. The doctors had told us that if it did, it would often come back with a different texture. Maybe even a different color. And I don't exactly know why, but the realization that his hair was falling out broke the emotional dam again. We sobbed as we watched him pick the hair out of his mac and cheese. After a few minutes we made the tough choice of a preemptive strike. We went on the offensive. It was our way of yelling back at cancer, "Nothing is going to take our son from us. We'll be the ones who decide what happens to his hair."

I found the hospital directory tucked away in a drawer and looked up the extension for the on-site barber. An hour later, armed with a set of stainless steel clippers, an elderly woman with a smoker's cough knocked on the door of our sixth floor room. Joshua sat on top of a booster seat in a wooden chair and the buzzing started. He thought it tickled. I didn't.

We told the barber to take off the guard—to get in as close as possible to his scalp. Then, stroke by stroke, his golden, almost white hair fell to the ground in great clumps rather than gradually into his food. Five minutes after the cutting started, it was over.

I've got to admit, he still looked pretty cute, at least to us.

We did notice, however, that the stares from the people we encountered outside the hospital dramatically increased. Suddenly they were confronted by the kid from the telethons but without a remote control in their hands to change the channel. The funny thing was that if not for Joshua's cue ball, there were moments we were almost able to forget about all the medication and the pain and the cancer. Sweet times of relaxing together as a family when he didn't have to move too much, putting a puzzle together on the floor or pushing him in a stroller on a walk. But then, just as we began to relax and really enjoy what was happening, we'd catch the glint of his head or the sideward glance of a passerby and remember.

Thorn

Remembering like that can be pretty jarring. It can keep you emotionally off balance, alternating between laughing and crying. Such an imbalance left me emotionally exhausted and numb, just feeling my way through each day. But in those rare reflective moments, I took comfort that feeling like that was probably something normal, that even a spiritual giant like Paul evidently knew what it was like to fluctuate between emotional extremes. At least that's what I took his description of the thorn in his flesh to mean.

I read Paul's mention of his thorn in the letter he wrote that's come to be known as 2 Corinthians. The word *skolops* in the Greek can mean "thorn," but it is sometimes translated *stake*. The word has a violent bent to it—*stake* doesn't strike up warm and fuzzy images in my mind when referring to pain. Indeed, the word *stake* conjures images of an almost savage pain. So the thorn in Paul's flesh wasn't a minimal, occasional pain but something that was always with Paul throughout his life. Wherever he went.

Some believe this ailment was severe headaches, and that would explain Paul's eye trouble he mentions at the close of the book of Galatians. Others say it was a recurring malaria fever that Paul picked up on one of his island adventures. If that's the case, then the thorn would be even more painful, for those suffering from that sort of fever have described pains in the head feeling something like a dentist's drill. Regardless of what the malady was, it was always there. No matter where he went, what he did, or how many people he led to the Lord, there was still this constant reminder of his own frailty.

Even here, in 2 Corinthians 12, Paul breaks out into a description of some glorious vision he had, a vision of heaven so amazing that he has to stand outside himself and say that it happened to another. He was enraptured. He experienced the fullness of joy, the essence of existence. He was living the greatness of eternity but not for long.

Imagine being caught up in that and then coming back to Earth. And then imagine that the thing that brings you back to Earth was the thorn. The pain. The ache. The sadistic dentist drilling ceaselessly into your head. That's a rude awakening but one I felt some kinship with. Both Jana and I were becoming well acquainted with the same feeling. It's the feeling of having life feel good, even normal, and then suddenly being brought crashing back to reality.

Trains

I'm not pretending I know how the apostle felt. I don't. I've never been caught up into a vision of heaven. And I've never had a ceaseless, boring pain in my head. But I know what it's like to forget about the pain for a bit only to be shocked back into reality. I know it because of the trains.

Joshua has always been a big fan of trains, especially everyone's favorite train from the island of Sodor. And during those days and weeks we spent in the hospital, we were thankful beyond words one morning to discover that at the end of the hallway, right next to the ever-elusive exit door to the outside world, was a playroom. And in the playroom was an enormous Thomas the Tank Engine train table. So every morning we would get up, get Joshua dressed in his ill-fitting clothes, and waddle down the hallway. Sometimes he would walk, but more times I carried him. His cheeks were red and flustered by the time we got there. The playroom didn't open until 10:00 a.m. most days, but we were there at 9:55, waiting. And if the lady with the key didn't come, we would search her out. When the door eventually opened, there were the trains. And there was my son, running to them. Hopping is probably a better description. He would stand there for hours, playing with the trains at the train table.

It was amazing. I would sit and read, or mess around on the computer, or get down and play a little myself. We would laugh, crash, and build. And we felt just like any other father and son, doing the same thing any other father and son might have been doing at the same moment. It felt exceedingly normal, and that felt exceedingly good. But then the beeping would start.

Although we were playing with trains, Joshua was almost constantly hooked up to an IV. And every couple of hours, we got to hear the infernal beeping. The beeping that wakes you in the night. The beeping when you're trying to have a meal. And the beeping that sends you crashing back to reality from a normal day of playing with trains. The beeping that with every shrill note reminds you, "You are not a normal father and son. Beep. Your little boy is hooked up to an IV. Beep. Your little boy has cancer. Beep." Not to compare myself with Paul, but I know a bit of what it's like to be suddenly brought back to the reality of a situation. And for the apostle, even in that description of the marvelous vision of paradise he experienced, the thorn was still there, bringing him back to Earth.

Or in our case there were the trains. The small moments of joy. The simple things that could almost make you forget what's happening. And then there was the beeping from the IV. Or the need for medication. Or the sudden pain in his belly. The thorn, reminding us all that we only have one foot in heaven.

Yes, *thorn* was a good word because it was indeed like having a thorn stuck in the bottom of your foot. You can sit down, relax, laugh, enjoy yourself, and completely forget it's there, but then you get up again. When you take a single step, you are immediately reminded that the pain is still there. It's occasionally forgettable but no less present.

Remission

What made the thorn worse in some ways was that we soon had real, legitimate reason to rejoice. About eight weeks after he began chemotherapy, Joshua entered remission. That was a big step and one we were grateful for. But up until we started walking through the path of cancer, we had a mistaken impression of what that meant. I used to think *remission* meant "done." Finished. Complete. But it doesn't. There is a large difference between being in remission and being cured.

Remission is the technical name for the state a person is in when the cancerous cells drop below a certain percentage of the overall cell count. But in the case of a childhood cancer, like leukemia, the treatment protocol is still three years long. *Three years.* Three years of oral chemotherapy every day. Three years of intravenous chemotherapy every four weeks through a port in his chest. Three years of chemotherapy injected into his spinal fluid via a spinal tap every twelve weeks. Three years. And for three years we lived very conscious of our humanity. There were moments of glory, like entering remission, but the pills or the calendar or the beeping always brought us back to Earth.

I suppose I shouldn't have been surprised at the tension between the moments of joy and the reminders of pain. Isn't that the nature of the human experience? The Christian experience? I think it is. Once we come to Christ, we have a new home, and it's not here. The Bible reminds us that we are going to experience trouble of all kinds here on Earth, and yet our ultimate treasure and citizenship is in heaven. But until we cross the Jordan and spend eternity with Jesus, we live here on Earth. Here where our bodies decay. Where suffering is a reality. Where little children have to take pills every day. It's like we have one foot in heaven and one foot firmly planted on Earth, and we live our lives between those two worlds. Between joy and pain. Between glory and dejection. Between elation and depression. Joshua, with his shining head and his beeping IV pole was simply living out that tension in a more visible form than most of us.

Sufficient

The good parts of living "in between" are many. Such a life makes you realize more and more that this earth is not your home, and you consequently begin to long for heaven. A life between develops perseverance and character that wouldn't have been there otherwise. And a life between forces you to a dependence on Jesus that you might not have chosen except for the pain.

That's all well and good, but when the IV machine started beeping, I found myself unconsciously slipping into a prayer for relief. Asking for a miracle. Begging, really. Just like Paul.

He asked the Lord, too. He asked him several times to take his thorn away. And he got back the same answer we did: No. This was going to be a long journey. A journey of years. There was to be no immediate relief of the pain, but as Paul discovered, that didn't mean the Lord was absent.

In the case of Paul's thorn, the request to remove it was denied, but an elaboration of the negative answer was given: "My grace is sufficient for you, for power is perfected in weakness" (2 Cor. 12:9).

The Lord had chosen for our family to live this portion of our lives as a visible demonstration of life "between." He was going to show His own strength through our weakness. The days when we were at the end of our rope were also the days when the sustaining grace and strength of God were to be most visible. He did not promise us that the pain would go away; but He promised that in the midst of it, His grace would be all that we needed.

We were left with the hard choice of believing that to be true. We had to choose to trust not in our own ability to be patient with a child on steroids, or even to get out of bed in the morning, but in the One who promised He would be strong in our stead.

But the great news of the gospel is that the power to sustain us comes from Jesus, who knows even better than we do what it is like to have one foot in heaven and one foot on Earth. Sustaining grace for life between comes from One who knows both the glory and the pain. It comes from One who knows the fullness of God and the fullness of man. It comes from One who was raised up on two crossbeams to where He was physically positioned not quite in the air and yet not quite on the earth either. It comes from One who knows what life is like in the "between." For when we look into the face of our Jesus, we rejoice, too, even in our thorns, because when we are weak, we are strong.

Jesus sustained us by His grace. We woke every morning, and the best way we knew how, knowing that the day would hold both moments of joy and moments of pain, we trusted in His strength. We trusted that He would be mighty in our weakness. And slowly something strange started to happen. It happened so slowly that we didn't even realize it until we were already neck deep into it. It was something that in the moment we were never sure would happen again. It was something that reminded us that God is for us. Slowly, but steadily, after a long time, Joshua's hair started to grow back.

Chapter 7

Recovery

Routines

We are creatures of routine. Even during something like chemotherapy treatments, you fall into a certain rhythm, and it becomes as normal as whether you wash your hair or your body first thing in the shower. That's both good and bad. On the bad side, routines often create a sense of boredom. They bring into our lives the temptation to consider everything as routine, as mundane. In a life like that, it's often difficult to stop and find the spiritual and extraordinary implications in what we consider to be normal.

But the good thing about a routine is that it establishes a sense of normalcy even when things in our lives are far from it. And that's healthy. That's what happened with us.

The days stretched into weeks, and the weeks stretched into months. And even with a two- and then three-year-old going through a regimen of chemotherapy, things became, well, normal. Or at least a version of normal.

In fact, they became so normal you could almost set your watch by it. Here's what our routine looked like: Every four weeks, on a Wednesday, Joshua went in for his dose of intravenous chemotherapy. On the way to the appointment, we drove through Starbucks, and he got a kid's hot chocolate. Then on to the hospital. The appointment took about three hours. Afterward, we went to lunch at a restaurant of Joshua's choosing, almost always some kind of deli where he could get a massive baked potato with no green onions and extra black olives.

That afternoon, we started his steroids. Wednesdays were pretty normal, though, as it took a while for the combined effects of the steroids and chemo to really hit his system. Thursdays started out like any other day, but by Thursday afternoon (around 3:00 p.m.), Joshua would start to get a little moody and tired. Then Friday the storm would blow in.

He woke up, not wanting to do anything but eat. The series of two or three breakfasts started, and he lay on the couch trying to get his strength under him for a few hours. Saturday was worse, though we planned small activities to get him out of the house for a while in order to distract him from his hunger and discomfort. Sunday was church day, and Joshua had a great time, though he was ravenous by the end. We finished Sunday evening with a family movie night, and he took his last dose of steroids. Monday the side effects were still visible, though starting to diminish. By Tuesday, at roughly 10:00 in the morning, he was back to himself. Then we would spend three and a half weeks like any other family. It was incredible how strictly his body stuck to this pattern.

I had the luxury of going to work in the midst of this routine. Jana, on the other hand, bore the brunt of the effects. Her routine started the week before a treatment week as she took a firm inventory of the snack supply in the house, making sure we had an ample selection and variety in order to quell the wrath of a steroid-induced fit. Having armed herself with a truckload of food, she set about making a list of activities exciting enough to take Joshua's mind off his discomfort and hunger and yet not strenuous enough to tax his little body. Sometimes the time was easy to fill. She and Joshua searched out each and every park within a twenty-five-square-mile area of our house, and they visited them all. They were quite a sight—a pregnant lady and a bald-headed child on either end of a teeter-totter.

Sometimes, though, she had to get creative. So there were trips to the random bookstore to read together. Or the daily ritual of walking to the unfinished end of our subdivision to throw rocks in the big puddle of water that always seemed to be there, right next to the houses under construction. She masterfully broke the day into thirty-minute segments, and in doing so, she was able to manage the time like a pro.

Joshua seemed to handle his own pain in a progressively better manner. Despite periodic outbursts of emotion or pain, eventually we reached a point when our family started to recognize that Joshua, as hard as it was to believe during those five days every four weeks, was in some sort of recovery. Joshua's hair wasn't fully grown back, and he still felt bad, and we still occasionally spent sleepless nights in the hospital. But he was indeed recovering. He was starting to run. He was starting to interact better with other kids. He was showing interest in the things any three-year-old boy would like. But though he was recovering, I was not.

I wasn't recovering from the emotional toll of childhood cancer. I wasn't recovering from my disjointed relationship with God. I wasn't recovering from my anger and fear. That's not to say, though, I didn't have my own pattern and routine. For three weeks I went to work, came home, played outside, rode bikes, and went to the pool. Then week four rolled around, and fear and anxiety began to creep back in.

Would this be the day we find out the cancer is back? How bad are the side effects going to be this time? How long can we emotionally sustain this? How long can we physically sustain this?

That's not to say the pattern was without benefit. It was

something to hang onto, and in a strange way, even comfortable. I believe I was mistaking a reliance and comfort level in that routine as my own recovery.

But it's not. Recovery is about moving forward and through the ailment. It's about the treatment that comes in order to make you a whole person again physically, or as much as can happen. My routine was really just another. coping mechanism, a tool that allowed me to function at a surface level while hiding from the fear, doubt, and anger that curdled down below. I was once full of dreams and hopes, and now I was full of . . . routine. Though I knew what to expect, even on treatment weeks, I still felt dry inside. Emotionally exhausted. Frayed at the edges.

I resonated greatly with Moses of the Old Testament, or at least to one part of his story. It's the part of the story that often gets lost in the midst of climbing the mountain of God, performing miracles in Egypt, and leading a train of captives out of bondage. Before all that, Moses spent forty years in the desert. And I suppose that in those forty years, he learned something about routine and hiding.

Before his time in the desert, Moses had great dreams, too. Educated and indoctrinated into the royal family of Egypt, Moses was raised in luxury. Despite that, he harbored aspirations of returning to his people as a great leader. In fact, he was so convinced that this was his destiny and God's purpose for his life that he killed an Egyptian taskmaster hoping to incite a rioting army of slaves to follow him. It didn't work.

Instead Moses ran from Egypt as a fugitive in disgrace. But the place he ran to is particularly interesting. He ran to the desert, just like me. Dry. Isolated. Frayed at the edges. The desert was a good place for both of us, just two guys living a life of "should have beens." Moses undoubtedly had lots of questions, maybe some anger, probably some bitterness. Spiritually Moses was in a dry, dry place. He was in a place filled with doubt and anxiety and sin; he was in a place far from the refreshing waters of the Lord.

Where better than the desert for him to gaze at the sky and ask, "I thought I was the deliverer? Why have you abandoned me? Why have you given me this vision for my people and then taken it away?" Where better than the desert for him to lose himself in the routine? Where better than the desert for him to forget about everything that might have been?

He ran into routine—a routine of tending sheep, an unceasing monotony that lasted four decades, but a great place to get lost and avoid engaging in those questions. I might have stayed in my own desert, tending my sheep and burying my real disappointment with God and fear of the future for the rest of my life. So might Moses, I guess. Neither of us were cooking up great schemes about how to get back into the proverbial promised land. But God took it on Himself to invade the routine of both the shepherd and the dad and force them both to stop hiding.

Bush

Moses went from the prince of Egypt to the bottom rung on the socioeconomic ladder, and he spent the next forty years of his life feeding sheep. And watering sheep. And protecting sheep. I don't know a lot about shepherding, but I would guess that it's pretty boring. Day after day, staring at the backsides of sheep for forty years. But on the plus side, he didn't have any daily reminders of what his life was "supposed" to be like. He had hidden, and he had hidden well. Maybe he had even talked himself into believing that he had recovered from what had happened in his life and had moved on to a regular, everyday existence. Moses had created a new normal for himself.

But then, on a day like any other, when the questions that had driven Moses to the desert in the first place had long since been pushed down into the pit of his soul, he chased a sheep up a mountain and everything changed.

A fire. A bush. A voice spoken on holy ground.

Moses was suddenly engaged by God. And isn't that always the way it happens? We trick ourselves into believing we have recovered when all we've really done is hid in the desert. But God is content to wait us out and then eventually to come storming into our lives all over again. We can never really hide from Him.

Something happens. We read something that should in no way make us as upset as we get. We see something that jars us emotionally. We smell something that reminds us of a time long ago. We encounter a bush on fire, and suddenly the wounds of the past—or at least those we thought were in the past—suddenly come to the surface. God finds us out because part of any type of recovery means confronting those issues and questions that drove us to the desert in the first place.

For Moses that invasion came in the form of a burning bush. For me it was Charlie.

Charlie

We met Charlie and his family on the sixth floor of the hospital. He had the same bald head as Joshua, and from the time they met each other they were often seen being pulled in a wagon together down the hallway. Or tottering on unsure legs toward as much adventure as that single floor could offer.

Charlie was about the same age as Joshua. He had a different type of leukemia, though—at least he did this time. His first bout with cancer was with the same type as Joshua, but then the unthinkable happened. After an extensive treatment of about a year, Charlie's mom and dad got a phone call at home one night telling them that he had relapsed. When we met them, they had started treatment over again for a different type of leukemia, one that would culminate in a dangerous bone marrow transplant.

That, however, did not seem to deter Charlie's zest for life. He and Joshua would chase each other down the hallways of the hospital, at least as fast as they could with me and Charlie's dad behind them pushing IV poles. They played baseball in the hallway with plastic bats and balls. Generally they had a good time because this was, for both of them, one of the only times they could be around children their own age without having to worry about compromising their immune systems. It was as if they had been thirsty for friendship and had finally found a well of water. And they drank deeply.

We prayed as Charlie prepared for his transplant and continued to pray that the new bone marrow would react positively with his existing blood. But in July, about ten months after Joshua's diagnosis, Jana and I got a babysitter and attended a memorial service for Charlie who had gone to be with Jesus a few days before.

It was one of the most difficult things I have ever had to do in my life. We joined a line of doctors, nurses, friends, and family all processing toward the front of the funeral home where Charlie's mom and dad stood shaking hands. Tracking around the edge of the room were pictures and toys that were special to their little boy. Charlie loved Buzz Lightyear; they had his Buzz costume at the front with a little sign below it that said, "To Infinity and Beyond." I wept at that, more so than the funeral or even talking to his parents. Then we got in the car and drove away.

I didn't want to, but I couldn't help thinking what pieces of stuff we would display at Joshua's funeral. Would it be his purple monkey, the one with the magnets stitched into the hands so that it could latch onto his IV pole and accompany him on his sixth floor adventures? His well-worn stuffed puppy, stained from two years of spit-up? His VeggieTales videos? His cars? His stick horse? A million little things that he loves. Maybe some airplane crackers or a fruit cup.

We drove home in silence, but my internal monologue was blazing: *Damn this disease and this world. Why children? Why Joshua? It's one thing to go to a funeral and reflect on a life well-lived, full of memories and time. Lots of time. But another thing entirely to go to a memorial service for a little boy. A little boy who barely knew how to love and hadn't yet made a single enemy. One who wasn't self-conscious enough to be embarrassed or prideful. And one who would never know.*

A burning bush. Holy ground. An encounter with God. And in the end I was asking the same question to God that Moses was: "Who are You?"

"I Am"

That was indeed how Moses responded to the burning bush. You would have thought he might have been more excited when God told Moses that his time in the desert had come to an end. Moses was going back—back to Egypt and back to his people. He was going to be the deliverer, the one to stand before Pharaoh and speak the word of the Lord. God had plans for his life, and the time had finally come for Moses to take hold of his destiny. Rise up, head back into Egypt! Except he wasn't excited. He was hesitant. And afraid.

He must have had fears that sounded remarkably similar to my own. Sitting in the desert, you don't have to think about weighty issues of evil and suffering. You don't have to confront just how broken and wounded you really are. But in that moment, Moses was tired of hiding. He bolstered his courage, screwed up his nerve, and asked the question that had long plagued him on the lonely desert nights: "Suppose I go to the Israelites and say to them, 'The God of your fathers has sent me to you,' and they ask me, 'What is His name?' Then what shall I tell them?"

But in this question Moses was doing much more than asking for a more familiar and intimate title for God. He wasn't asking for some secret password that only the Jews knew either. The name Moses is looking for is not just a title—God had already given that. Moses wanted to know who God is . . .

really. That was the significance of the name to the culture of the day. It was the one-word summation of a person's character—a description of what makes them who they are. When he asked, "What is Your name?" He was really asking, "Who are You to promise deliverance? Can You really do what You say You can? Are you really able? Let's get to the meat of it: Who are You *really?*"

This isn't just *a* question; it is *the* question. It was the same question building inside of me. *Who are You?*

Up to that point I thought I knew. I was so sure of myself. But in the wake of Charlie's funeral, having been pushed out of my comfortable routine and forced to confront the deep issues of grief and loss, I no longer was certain.

Who are You?

It was not a question of theological debate. It was not an ivory-tower query. This was the question of emotionally brutalized princes-turned-shepherds. It was the same question God's people, the Israelites, were asking in their own pain, given that they had been praying for relief and deliverance for four hundred years. It was the question of a father trying to hold life together, driving home from a memorial service for a little boy that looked far too much like his own son. But it was also the question God Himself draws out of you when He's not content for you to live in the desert any more.

God's response? "I am who I am."

That is a strange way to respond because the name God calls Himself by is the present tense of the verb "to be." God said to tell the people that He is. He is the one who is. Or He is the "Is-ing" One. He is "be." And while confusing at first, it was evidently motivational enough for Moses to pick up his staff and continue on. He moved out of his coping mechanisms; embraced his doubt, disappointment, and pain; and put one foot in front of the other.

I wanted to do the same thing. And I began to see that in this answer is a fundamental truth about God that could radically alter the way I moved forward into true recovery.

God, our God, is the God who is. He is not the God who was, and He is not the God who will be, but He is the God who is. This God who is the Creator of time exists outside of its boundaries. To Him there is no past. No future. Everything is right now. He is the God of the present, and the present is important to those experiencing pain and loss.

The reason it's so important is that the "right now" was precisely what I was hiding from in the desert. I was burying myself in work or church or writing or whatever—anything to keep me from existing in the moment. I was working so hard at doing so because I knew that in the moment it hurt. Everything hurt. And I was tired of hurting. It was much easier to push away the truth of life as it was—that I was struggling in my job, that my son had cancer, and that I was floundering in the world.

But God would not allow that. It's against His character, a violation of His name. God is the God of now, and for me that meant owning up to the truth of right now and all the turmoil that went with it.

Now

Because God is the God who is, He can bend down and weep because He lives in the present. He is the God who can sympathize in your every trial and temptation because He lives in the now. But most of all, He is the Father who knew His Son to be the lamb slain before the foundation of the world because He lives in the now. And Jesus Christ is the same as yesterday and today and forever because He is the One who is. God's response to Moses is the same to anyone living in the desert: "You may think I'm absent. You may have questions about the way your life is going. But I have not left you. In fact, I'm with you even now in that desert you are calling home. I am present in your pain, for I am the God who is."

My son with cancer understands what it means to live in the now better than I do. Joshua doesn't keep a calendar. He didn't recognize when week four rolled around and it was time for his treatment again. He didn't even care that he was going to feel bad after he went to the hospital because Joshua lives in the moment. He does not live with a sense of dread of tomorrow or a sense of nostalgia about the past because he knows how to be in the moment. And that's why, on a Tuesday before he gets poison pumped into his body the next morning, Joshua is ready to go swimming. Or play Star Wars. Or hit baseballs. He is doing the very thing we are admonished to do in the Sermon on the Mount—to not worry about tomorrow. Instead, we are to trust in God's provision during the "right now" and worry about tomorrow when it becomes "right now." Indeed, tomorrow is "right now" to Him already.

Recovery is just that. No more escaping. No more hiding in the desert. No more wishing for the past and just trying to get to the future. Recovery is about right now. And the God who is right now reminds us that we don't have to stay in the desert. We have strength for today because He is. He is never the God who used to be. And He's never the God who might be someday. He is. Just as in the past, when He was "is" then. And when the hard times come tomorrow, He'll be present then too because He always is. Live in the present. Rejoice in the present. Cry in the present. Be fully alive in the present, because He is "I am."

Chapter 8

Together

Tired

It's hard to be friends with "those people." I know because we are "those people." When you're in relationship with someone and then something world-shaking happens to them—job loss, diagnosis, infidelity, whatever—it casts a looming shadow over every interaction you have with them. You may still have dinner together or go to the movies, but in the background you know that in the back of their mind is a crumbling marriage, a battle with depression, or in our case chemo drugs in the medicine cabinet. Though you want to "be there" for them, whatever that means, it's an extraordinarily difficult task. How do you ask about the elephant in their lives? Do they even want to talk about it?

How can you show empathy when you've never experienced what they are experiencing?

It's exhausting to be in that kind of relationship. You can have only so many conversations around the serious, mind-blowingly difficult nature of life circumstances until you just get tired of doing so. Every time you spend a few moments with "those people," it seems like they need to cry. Or they're closed off emotionally. Or they have nothing to say about their kid with cancer. Exerting that kind of effort just makes you tired. So who can blame you when, after a while, you just sort of drift out of their lives? You find yourself unable to relate to them any more, and all the emotional energy you have put forth toward the relationship makes you just need a break.

At least that's what we saw.

As Joshua's treatment stretched from days to weeks to months and then eventually to years, it was interesting to step back and look around at how the dynamics of our relationships changed over time. It was no one's fault really, but some with whom we once were so close drifted out of our lives. It was a subconscious drifting for both parties.

From their perspectives I think they just didn't know how to interact with us anymore. We were the people who had to shut ourselves off from the world for almost a year due to our son's suppressed immune system that made him unable to be around other children for fear of his catching something. We were the people who countless times had to call and cancel plans because Joshua was feeling bad or we were in the hospital again. We were the people who seemed to be always in need and so were constantly taking from our relationships. And that taking was one of the hardest things for us.

I didn't intend to be selfish and egocentric about Joshua's cancer. It was, after all, about him and not me. But I found myself with an increasing inability to relate to other people's struggles, internally thinking, *You think you've got it bad . . .* Relationships must be about both giving and taking, depending on a person's season of life, and I was a taker. Ironically, my taking made me increasingly isolated. I rarely brought up our situation in conversation, and I spent more and more time by myself. But at the same time I was sequestering myself, I found that I secretly, at least at some level, enjoyed the fact that people knew my son had cancer. When I knew they knew, I didn't have to talk about it. But I also relished in the fact that I seemed to have some unearned measure of respect and even admiration because of my life situation. I was the guy who knew what it meant to struggle, and my isolation only added to the mystique of my personality, as if I spent all day brooding over the deep issues of suffering and evil in the world. I didn't, but it was OK with me that people thought I did. So you see how there's enough blame to go around; people around us withdrew, and that was just fine with me.

Isolation was an easy fit for me. As an introvert I am drained by being around people for long periods of time. My natural reset status is by myself, so the fact that I was withdrawing struck me as a pretty comfortable place to be. But something else made it comfortable, too.

Isolation was also easy because of my rugged, American individualism. I grew up reading history books and watching movies about self-made men and women. These were the forgers of culture and society, the individuals who had enough intestinal fortitude to go at it alone. They were the leaders of the pack, whether in sports, technology, or government; and when the odds were stacked against them, they somehow found the strength inside themselves to keep going.

Alone.

Indeed, in our culture that's the true mark of strength—what you can do by yourself. That same idea has strongly influenced North American Evangelical Christianity, the kind of faith I was holding onto when Joshua was diagnosed. Alongside these epic tales of the strength of the individual, I had heard countless people talk about my "personal relationship with Jesus Christ." Part of what I heard in that terminology was that the way I related to God sat on my shoulders. Me. An individual.

In my mind, then, the true test of strength in life, spiritual or otherwise, was my ability to take issues on my own shoulders and deal with them. Other people were OK to have around, but in the end it was up to me. If I couldn't handle something myself, it was a tick on my record, a mark of my own weakness and inadequacy. And I was adequate.

I did not need anyone. I did not even want anyone. So if they were tired of being around me and my family—"those people"—that was fine. I was tired, too. Fortunately there were people in my life who didn't share that opinion.

Burden Barriers

If we were "those people," there were "those other people" in our lives. "Those other people" are annoying to "those people" because they're the ones who refuse to drift. They're the ones who push through the awkwardness. They're the ones, even when you don't have anything to say, who are content to let you have nothing to say and are even OK with the silence between you. These were the people who stayed and refused to allow me to slip farther into isolation. And in time I grew to see that life together, especially during times of pain, is exactly the way God designed it.

These people never had T-shirts made, but if they had, I think embroidered on the back would have been a slogan that read something remarkably similar to Galatians 6:2: "Carry one another's burdens; in this way you will fulfill the law of Christ."

In Galatians, you actually find two words for *burden*. One of the words implies a picture of a small knapsack that is light and portable, something a soldier might wear to be mobile. The other word, the one used in this verse, is different. The etymology of the word *burden* in verse 2 implies a heavy weight or stone that someone has to carry for a long time. It refers to something so ridiculously large and cumbersome that it is absurd to think that someone could carry it alone. Specifically, in this passage the burden in question is sin. But Paul knew the issue was deeper. So did I. Carrying another person's burdens means helping to shoulder that which is far too heavy to be carried alone. Things like a sick child. Whether I wanted to admit it or not, the burden was heavy.

Heavy like a boulder. Heavy like a boulder that must be moved a great distance. According to Galatians, the proper response to a burden like that isn't to suck it up, chalk your hands, and get busy lifting. In short, it wasn't to live like I was trying to live. The proper response is to spread out the burden over the shoulders of those around you and lift together. In this way a group of people actually becomes the church—a group of people understanding that when something happens to one of us, it happens to all of us, and therefore we are committed to walking through the difficulties of life humbly together.

Great idea, but unfortunately, that was completely counter to every instinct inside me. I mean, the whole meaning behind "that's just my cross to bear" implies that we are on this journey by ourselves, and the measure of our maturity is how much we can handle alone. And if that's true, the true measure of one's weakness and immaturity is the inability to deal with their own stuff. Consequently, if all was visible that is now invisible, we would see countless members of the body of Christ with stooped shoulders and sweat-beaded foreheads, desperately trudging through life echoing the mantra, "I'm doing fine."

But we are not fine. None of us is. I certainly wasn't. But despite that "not-fineness," and despite the weight of the burden, I wanted nothing less than to have someone help me carry it. I didn't want to open up. I didn't want to share. It's strange to say, but when you live with pain, you almost begin to have a relationship with it. I hated that my son had cancer, but in some strange way I found myself clinging to it at the same time. That was my burden—mine—and no one was going to take it from me.

I longed for the days when I was able to help others shoulder their load. That's a much more comfortable position for me—to hear the confession, to hand out the Kleenex, and to put my best "counselor" face on. But I found the idea insulting that someone was going to do that for me. I didn't need that. I was above it.

But these other people were not to be deterred. They bombarded me with kindness and compassion. They wouldn't leave well enough alone and always seemed to be handing me a gift card for a restaurant or mowing my grass. There was a steady stream of visitors to the hospital and invitations to get cups of coffee. These were the people who started carrying Purell in their pockets so they could wash their hands as they came into our house. They made Joshua a DVD of his favorite cartoons to watch in his room by himself. They spent the night in the hospital so Jana and I could sleep in the same bed. And slowly but surely, I found myself breaking under the onslaught of their attacks. The burden didn't get lighter, but it did get more evenly distributed.

It's an amazing thing to see people, who are not related to you in anyway other than through the blood of Jesus, weep tears for your child when your own tears have long since dried up. It was as if they had taken Joshua into their own hearts and families so deeply that they were becoming a legitimate part of our own family. We hurt and they hurt. We laughed and they laughed. We lifted, and thank God, they lifted, too.

But the most powerful memory I have of those days when these people taught me what it meant to shoulder the weight of another isn't some wise words of counsel. Nor was it some grand act of service or generosity that made the medical bills go away. Instead, it was the simple act of watching a baseball game.

World Series

We are a baseball family. Jana loves the Atlanta Braves, mainly because theirs were the only games televised in her New Mexico town growing up. So she and her dad would sit on the couch, and he would dispense the wisdom of an ex-catcher about pitches, batting stances, and hit and runs.

I played baseball growing up, too, and I've got my own memories of watching Nolan Ryan pitch live for the Texas Rangers during his final season in Arlington. So when late September and October roll around, we start listening to sports radio a little more closely. We start planning our nights and weekends around league championship series. Our meals subtly shift toward hot dogs, nachos, and Frito pie. And when the World Series comes around, we gather with friends and families and watch the games in our home. We wanted to do it again.

But like so many things in the life of a cancer-stricken family, those plans were derailed by yet another hospital stay. We wouldn't be laughing and cheering in our own home that year; we'd be sleeping separately from each other again in the hospital. To anyone else it might have seemed like no big deal. And it really wasn't, I guess. But in that moment, to Jana and me, it was just another in a long line of disappointments. Another reminder that our lives were being dictated to us by a disease. And that's when those people stepped in.

On the night of game one, they were there. In the hospital waiting room. With hot dogs and cheese sauce and chips in tow. They sat in that waiting room alongside us, necks craned upward and eyes squinting at the baseball game on the small mounted television set in the upper corner of the room. There was no talk of cancer. There were no words of advice. No tears were shed. There was just, for a night, a group of friends watching a ball game as they might have done on any other October night.

None of that mattered because these people had something better than advice. They showed up. That night as we watched the tiny TV, I realized that this was one of the essences of true community—just showing up. Day after day. Night after night. They refused—*refused*—to go away. These are the lifters of burdens, not the fixers of problems. They made both Jana and me remember a quote from Henri Nouwen in his book *The Road to Daybreak: A Spiritual Journey*: "When we honestly ask ourselves which person in our lives mean the most to us, we often find that it is those who, instead of giving advice, solutions, or cures, have chosen rather to share our pain and touch our wounds with a warm and tender hand." They practiced the ministry of presence that night in the hospital waiting room. By just showing up, these good people served as a tangible reminder of the invisible realities of God that during times of pain we are so prone to forget.

Remembering

Pain hurts, but it also dulls our memories. It increases our already large propensity to forget the fundamental truths of the faith we know to be true. During those times of suffering, we feel most alone. We feel the most forgotten. We feel the most forsaken. Through the people continuing to show up, we can be reminded of our God. Our God who loves us. Our God who is in control. Our God who cares deeply and walks with us. Our God who bends low to weep in the dirt.

In a sense you could say that the church is a string around its own finger.

When I couldn't believe that God was still with us, my memory was jogged by the persistent presence of others. When I was tempted to forget that God cared deeply for us, the tears of our friends made His love more real. When I thought the world was spinning out of control, the calm assurances of the people that stayed reminded me of a God who has a purpose and a plan. This, I think, is the truth John wrote about in 1 John 4:11–12: "Dear friends, if God loved us in this way, we also must love one another. No one has ever seen God. If we love one another, God remains in us and His love is perfected in us."

It's not as if God's love is deficient in some way, that He needs us to put His love over the top. Rather, when we show up for one another, the invisible reality of the love of God becomes visible among us. Our friends reminded me of what my drift into isolation threatened to make me forget: God never stops showing up.

In the kingdom of God, we are meant to take responsibility for one another. It's not one person versus the world. We are meant to live life not as one but as many. We are the body of Christ. Together, that's why we show up for each other—it's because in Jesus, we have been inseperably joined through our common faith in the gospel. When one, like me, wants to slip away into oblivion, God's solution isn't necessarily a miraculous end to the pain but rather that those people around them can remind them of the invisible realities of God. And we all need reminding from time to time. That's why we live life together.

Chapter 9

Hope

Heaven

Hope, by its very nature, has an element of pain associated with it. That's why we hope at all. If everything were perfect in our present circumstances, then what would we have to hope for? So when you hope, you are implicitly acknowledging that something in your experience isn't as it should be. Or as it will be (so you hope). I suppose we never truly lost hope. On the days when Joshua was too tired and sick to get off the couch, we knew that in a few days the worst chemo would be flushed out of his system. When Jana and I were both exhausted from two-hour sleeping increments in the hospital, going to work, and then doing it all over again, we had the feeling that the pattern couldn't last forever. The sores would eventually heal. Joshua would be able to bend his legs without pain again. And we would eventually rest. Even on the darkest days, we held on to the knowledge in the back of our minds that things were going to be OK, even if it didn't happen until we got to heaven.

But is that the real nature of hope? Is hope simply the idea . . . the longing . . . the feeling deep inside you that things are going to get better? If that's the case, then living in hope can easily turn into a starry-eyed gazing upon supposed future events when things are set right and as they should be. And I guess that's part of it.

Heaven, after all, is a realm in which we don't need Kleenex, hearses, or chemotherapy any more. As I lay next to Joshua in his hospital bed, I longed for heaven. When I watched him being pumped full of chemicals. When I was powerless to take away any of his pain. But heaven goes beyond physical and emotional relief. It's a place where we know God as He knows us, fully and completely. It's a place where we will no longer struggle with sin, a place where faith is no longer needed because what we hope for will be our reality. That's definitely part of it. But here's the problem with that:

You only go to heaven when you die.

That's an elemental truth but a hard one to swallow because it means there are a lot of things we are hoping for that we'll never see this side of the Jordan. Or to put it another way, some things aren't going to get better. In fact, many things will get worse. Our bodies, our health, the world, the level of morality—these things aren't trending in a positive direction. And that has big implications in exactly what we are hoping for.

It would be much easier to hold on to the easier form of hope, that whatever bad is happening in life is just happening for a season and things are bound to get better someday. Someday before we die. Someday soon. That's a much more comfortable hope to have, though it might be grounded in at least some measure of naivety.

Given, then, that things might not get better in the immediate future or even at all until we look Jesus in the face, we might be tempted to fall into despair, just waiting for the sweet relief of heaven. But just as the hope that "things are bound to turn around eventually" seems naive, the just-waiting-to-die kind of hope seems morbid and contrary to how Jesus would want us to live. Isn't there an element of hope that is for this life and not just the next one? If God is indeed the God of hope, then can't we place our hope in something right now? That's really what I was longing for. It's great that heaven is out there in the future, but I wanted—*needed*—hope in the present.

Wandering

Hoping is a struggle. It's a choice to hope, especially during a time when you feel like your whole life has been put on hold.

That's sort of what we felt like when we were sequestered in our house. For the first eight months, we had little to no contact with the outside world. No church. No preschool. No playdates. No McDonald's playground. That was a big one. For more than three years, every time we went through a drive-through at a fast-food joint with a playground, Joshua looked longingly out the window. After about a year and a half, he quit asking if he could play on it. But without fail I looked into the backseat and saw him there, his little hands clasped in front of his face, tears just below the surface. Our avoidance was due to Joshua's depressed immune system and the need to keep him safe. Indoor playgrounds are petri dishes for disease and were to be avoided at all costs. We found ways to amuse ourselves around the house, but on the whole it felt like we had pressed "pause" on our lives. And though we were excited to push "play" again, we knew that doing so had another set of challenges with it.

When we reengaged with the world, how would we be different? How would Joshua be different? Given the amount of time he spent in bed, how physically and socially behind other kids his age would he be? We worried about all these issues, and yet we tried to cling to the hope that we could be a normal family, whatever that means.

It was the feeling of being paused between the memory of the past and the hope of the future. A feeling of "lostness" dominated my mind and heart, and I felt like there, in the middle of the past and future, I was wandering around in circles—that there was a better destination out there somewhere, and yet in the meantime I was chasing my tail. During those days—those "paused" days—I felt like the nation of Israel must have felt. They, I knew from my seminary days, were familiar with being caught in the middle of two periods of time.

I wonder if there were any Israelites who would have found my internal monologue as a match to their own. I thought often about the carefree days of the past and longed for the hopeful days of the future. Surely they must have done the same thing, for there was a period in the history of that nation when the past was lost to them and the promised future was not yet upon them.

Those people spent a good chunk of time living in exile. That was after the glorious days of their past, when God had delivered them into the promised land, and before the hopeful days of the future when the prophets had told them there would be a new age of Messianic blessing. In the meantime, though, not much was good. They were far from home, biding their time until the pagan nation that had conquered them would be overthrown and they might return to the land promised to them by God. There, in Babylon, captive to a foreign people, surely they must have had questions like mine.

They must have known, just as I did, that things would never be the way they were again. Cancer had marked us—it had changed us—and I wasn't sure if we would ever recover. Not really. Similarly, the land of those captive Hebrews was in shambles. Their temple was destroyed. The priesthood was in disarray. The monarchy was disgraced. Every mark of favor the Lord had given to His people was removed, and the Israelites found themselves in a time when the foundations of their entire existence had crumbled. I get that. I could almost hear their unspoken questions as they sat in Babylon because they were the same ones filling my head:

Can things ever be as they were again?
What does the future hold for us?
Are we going to die in exile?

That's the nature of being caught, whether by cancer or by an invading army, in the meantime—that place between how things used to be and how they might be again.

Meantime

This is the nature of the meantime. It is that time when you have graduated from college, but the job market is dried up so you find yourself working two or three jobs just to get by. It is that time after one relationship ends and another one begins. It is when you have moved back in with your parents until you can find a place of your own. The meantime is the time after things were really good but before they get good again. In our case the meantime was that period after Joshua had gone into remission but before he was done with treatment and declared to be cured. And we asked a lot of the same questions.

Surely things were never going to be like they were again. We had been marked and wounded by this part of our journey, and there's no going back to the precancer days. In fact, we will be visiting the hematologist at least once a year until Joshua is eighteen years old. We'll always be watching him for little signs that might point to relapse. The old days are gone. And the future? Well, we dreamed about what life would be like when Joshua wasn't taking upwards of fifteen pills a week, when he wasn't having poison injected into his body every four weeks, and when he didn't have a lump in his chest from the implanted port. We dreamed about doing things like playing on the slide at McDonalds, and our eyes filled with tears. But those things were long in the future. The meantime was a sense of guarded optimism, the hope that things will get better but the fear that they won't.

That's how I felt. But I wondered: *Is this how I am supposed to feel? Is this the nature of hope? What would God say, if anything, to someone like me caught between the past and future? What am I supposed to think? What does it mean to hope when you're scared to do so?* I came to believe that God's Word for that time in my life was the same word that came from the mouth of the prophet Jeremiah to the exiled Israelites. So I read about the message for that time and found, as difficult as it was, that the words rang true for me, too.

Strap In

At first glance Jeremiah's words were comforting. Very comforting, in fact. For one of the most famous verses in the Bible came to people feeling exactly like I was, and it seemed that God didn't want any of us to live devoid of hope. So Jeremiah spoke through the passage of time the same words of encouragement he gave to his own people:

> *"'For I know the plans I have for you,'—this is the* LORD'*s declaration—'plans for your welfare, not for disaster, to give you a future and a hope.'" (Jer. 29:11)*

Unfortunately, the rest of what he said wasn't quite as palatable. I wanted God's message to be something like this: "Hang in there; it's almost over. The meantime won't last long. I'm about to return everything you have lost, and pretty soon you can move into the future." But that's not what He said. God refused, both then and now, to give some pie-in-the sky version of hope that denies the pain of the present. He was real in His words.

The word of the Lord reads something like this: "It's going to be seventy years of meantime, friends. It's going to be so long in the meantime that I advise you to get used to it. Settle down and make a life in the meantime. Build a house in the meantime because you are going to be there for a while. So strap in."

That wasn't great news. How many times I have wished that we might just wake up one day and chemo would be over. Joshua would be cured. The medicine would have been "miracled" out of the cabinet. But it wasn't. Nothing seemed to change. Day after day we woke up and gave our son chemotherapy pills to chew up in tablet form. Day after day we saw kids his age running around, but we saw them from the confines of our house. Day after day we wondered if today was the day we would get the call that the cancer was worse or something had changed in his prognosis.

And that's the way it's going to happen for most of us—no immediate miracle. No mind-blowing display of the power of God. No instant removal of the rogue blood cells. Whatever brought about these circumstances, we're probably going to be in this in-between season for a long time. That's a difficult thing to stomach.

Certain strains of theology claim that existing in this in-between time is not God's will for anyone's life. That God's design is for you never to be poor, hurting, sick, or desperate. And if you find yourself in such a situation, the problem is with your faith. If you really believed strongly enough, then God would change your circumstances. Through the power of positive thinking, God will make you healthy, wealthy, and wise. That was the opinion of one guy I met when I was traveling in Texas. He was a decent guy, and I enjoyed being around him; but through our interactions over the course of a weekend, I sensed he wanted to talk to me about something.

Finally, as he was driving me to the airport, he got around to it. In a polite way he came to his point at last—if I really believed, Joshua would be healed. Indeed, what I should be doing wasn't seeking treatment but repenting of my disbelief so that God would spring into action. I wanted to punch him.

In my more sarcastic moments, I can't help but wonder how the ten of the first twelve disciples who died in brutal ways would have felt about such theological toilet paper. But it does raise an interesting question: Why does God leave us in the meantime for so long?

Battling cancer is a process that takes years. A person might job hunt for months and months and never find anything. Couples can try and try to conceive a child only to come up with nothing. Godly men and women might wait to run into their future spouse and never go on a date. Why doesn't God deliver? It would be tempting for us to look at the amount of time we spend in the meantime and despair. We might even begin to think that God is like a kid with a magnifying glass in the sky burning ants out of sadistic pleasure down here on the earth, that He perversely enjoys watching humanity suffer. But maybe something deeper than that is going on here.

Complete

Think about the ministry of Jesus. Jesus healed and helped a lot of people. Blind people saw, deaf people heard, dead people lived. But not all of them. Not everyone in the crowds was touched. Not everyone threw away their crutches. Not everyone got their miracle. Lots of people walked (or hobbled) away from Jesus disappointed. Now unless we believe that Jesus just picked people out of a crowd at random to help, then some kind of divine wisdom and methodology must be guiding Him to who would receive that immediate, tangible healing. And conversely, there must be a divine intentionality to those who didn't get it. We were those people.

As in all such things, we should tread pretty carefully when making statements like, "This is why God does so and so," but it does seem that in the case of the crowds, Jesus healed immediately and publicly in order to establish His credentials. He healed, proving His divinity, and therefore adding validity to His words and actions. Those instances are plain, visible proof of the power of Jesus as God. That's not to say Jesus wasn't motivated out of compassion for the individual, but it does begin to get at why we cannot let our hope rest on this kind of immediate exit from the meantime.

Jesus was more than capable of healing everyone He came in contact with. Likewise, He was more than capable of eradicating cancer from my little boy's body. But He didn't. And maybe that's because, in His wisdom, He knew that doing so immediately and publicly would be, in some way, short-changing the ultimate healing He wanted to accomplish.

Living in the meantime has brought to light diseases I didn't know I had. It's brought to light my shallowness. It's brought to light my idealistic view of faith. It's brought to light my dependence on circumstances and my reluctance to accept responsibility. It's brought to light my love of all things material. Had Jesus chosen to heal Joshua immediately and pluck us from the grip of the meantime, these diseases would have remained firmly implanted in my heart and soul. But because of the time we have had to trudge through this battle, I have come to know (and in many cases, repent) of things I might not ever have been cognizant of otherwise.

From that perspective, Jesus' refusal to heal immediately is really His commitment to longer, better, and more complete healing—not just for Joshua but for me, too. So while I cannot place my hope in circumstances changing immediately or even inside of seventy years in the case of the Israelites, we can hope in something else. Namely, while we might feel pain and frailty and uselessness in the meantime, and while the Israelites might have enough time there to build a house and marry off a daughter, God is busy. That's the good news from Jeremiah.

Busy

The good news for us was not, "It's almost over," or "Just hang in there a little longer." He didn't urge us to put hope in the change of circumstance. In fact, He said the opposite. He said to live life. Build houses. Plant fields. Celebrate marriage. Really live. For us, that meant recognizing we were going to be dealing with cancer for a long time, but we also had to live our lives. And living life meant we were going to be parents again. Our second child's arrival was imminent, but we had little time or emotional energy to invest in preparation. Yet there was a little girl on the way, a growing reminder that God is in the business of making new things all the time. And in Jana's progression through pregnancy with our second child, we saw real hope. It's not believing circumstances will change because the truth is they might not for a long time. Or ever. Hope is the confidence that even during the meantime God is still busy.

Even in the meantime God was still dreaming about our lives. Nothing seemed more unlikely for the exiled Israelites in Babylon—from the meantime. In Babylon you feel forsaken. You feel forgotten. You feel lost. But God knew the plans He has for us, even though we were in the meantime. Those are plans to prosper us, not to harm us. Those are plans to give us a hope and a future, even though we were stuck in Babylon. No matter how confused or forgotten we felt in that in-between part of life, God never stopped dreaming about our futures. He didn't stop dreaming about what we were becoming. The meantime is an awful time to be in, but it's the perfect time for "becoming."

In those moments of pain, weakness, and tragedy, God does the hard work of bringing out the true nature of what ails you. He exposes who you really are and sets about the hard work not only of healing your son but of setting you on a course of becoming something different than you are. Becoming more patient. Becoming more faithful. Becoming more like Jesus. That's what we can hope in—the complete healing from God that results not in a destination of perfect comfort but in becoming.

Believing that God is at work does not deny the darkness of the present. It's not turning a blind eye to the evil of the world. And it's not a pie-in-the-sky view of the future, believing that if you just hang on, things are going to get better. Real hope is grounded in reality, and the ultimate truth of reality is that we are loved by a busy God—One who never stops working in us.

No one knows the nature of true hope better than Jesus Himself, for He knows what it's like to be in a circumstantially hopeless situation. He knows what it's like to live in the three longest days of meantime in the history of the cosmos. Those were days of nails and crossbeams. They were days of crowns of thorns and spears in the side. But even on that darkest of days, the Father knew the plans He had for the Son—plans to prosper Him and not to harm Him, plans for hope and a future. Even during the meantime after the crucifixion, God was dreaming about Sunday morning and His Son rising again. And if He was dreaming during those days, surely it's not too much to believe that He still might be planning and working and dreaming during our meantime.

We chose—are choosing—to hope in that. We're still trying like crazy not to make our hope purely circumstantial but to hope instead in the wisdom, compassion, and love of a busy God. But we have to choose to do so. We have to fight to do so, especially from the context of the meantime. We must choose to believe that God has not stopped dreaming and making plans for our lives, that His goodness is bigger than our circumstances.

So in May, seven months after we first heard the word *leukemia,* we named our daughter Andi.

Andi Hope.

Chapter 10

Faith

Blood

As a Christian, I've heard about blood for a long time. At a cursory glance through the Bible, you would find more than four hundred appearances of the word. Blood of cows, blood of goats, blood on the altar, blood in food, and the blood of Jesus. The Bible has much to say about that. The blood of Jesus is what covers the life of the believer. His blood makes atonement for our sin. The way this happens is a great mystery in a lot of respects. We know some things about the process, though. We know, for example, that without blood there is no remission of sin. And we know that all the blood that for centuries was poured on the altars of Israel was really just a shadow leading up to the one-time distribution of the blood of the Son of God. And we know that He bled so we don't have to. He was wounded so we might be forgiven. He was punished so we might have peace.

Blood is important to the Christian. But as the months ticked on in Joshua's treatment, I gained an ever-increasing knowledge of not only the spiritual but the physical significance of blood. It seems simplistic to say, but blood is important. Blood is essential. Blood fuels everything else. Blood is what flows out of you, signaling a significant injury; and blood is what's put back into you in order to sustain life. In many ways that's what blood is—the essence of life, both in a physical and a spiritual sense. And in the case of leukemia, blood was the focus of every trip to the clinic.

When Joshua was first diagnosed, the doctors needed to know how far his cancer of the blood had advanced, and so they took a bone aspiration from his hip and tested it. The test revealed that 86 percent of his blood cells were cancerous. That still feels like an enormous number. It was; the doctors started chemotherapy immediately. On the day after his diagnosis, Joshua began the endless regimen of injections, spinal taps, and pills that would last for more than three years. But instead of doing that painful bone biopsy each time we visited the clinic, the first order of business was a blood test.

Every time Joshua visited the clinic after his diagnosis (which numbered close to one hundred by the end of three years), we could count on the fact that right out of the gate, he would have blood drawn. That blood would be tested. Then the doctors would read the levels of the red and white blood cells in that blood, and those numbers would indicate whether or not the chemo was doing its job. So we learned the language of lymphoblasts and neutropenia and white counts. We began to understand ANCs and transfusions and remission. We learned more about blood than we ever thought possible. Certainly more than we ever wanted to know.

We would arrive at the hospital for Joshua's regular chemotherapy appointment (or whenever else he might get a little sick) and sit in the waiting room until we were called into the blood room. Then his port—a small, circular pad inserted in his chest—would be accessed, and the blood would be drawn. Then we'd start his chemotherapy drip and wait for the results.

Most of the time it was completely uneventful, and the biggest problem we had was when some other family had already laid claim to the best toys in the playroom or were monopolizing the television. The doctor would eventually walk out from the back set of offices holding a single, 8½ x 11 piece of white paper that contained a printout of Joshua's blood levels. They would talk us through the readings of the day, and we would dutifully nod.

It all amounted to the fact that the chemo was working.

Because we did this at least every four weeks, sometimes more than once a week, the initially intimidating process became comfortable. We knew all the nurses by name, and Joshua knew how to hold up his shirt and wait for the needle prick. I can still recite the way the nurses explained the insertion of the needle and the tube that was left dangling from his chest in order to administer the chemotherapy: "Now we stick your magic button, and there's the tubie. Now we use the pillow (gauze) and a blanket (large bandage) to make sure it doesn't move."

Through the first fifty appointments or so, I was nervous when I saw the doctor walking toward us with that white sheet of paper. *What would it say today?* But then I began to settle into a kind of passive expectation that passed for faith.

Here comes Dr. Zeiber. Now she's going to hand us the counts. Now she will talk to us about Joshua's ANC. It's either going to be reasonably high, meaning we can do some things in the germ-filled public, or it's going to be low because of the chemotherapy. In that case we'll have to go through the drive-through on the way home instead of eating inside.

That's how it was, and I suppose you could call that faith on my part. But it really wasn't. It was really just that I thought I knew exactly what was coming. My familiarity with the process, combined with the fact that we had every indication that the chemotherapy was doing its job, supplanted the desperation that requires constant belief in the provision of God. It was a passivity of faith; it was belief that had morphed into assumption. The apprehension had passed, and I stopped thinking about relapse.

But then it all changed.

Relapse

About eighteen months after Joshua was diagnosed, I went to work and Jana found herself sitting in that same waiting room where we had grown comfortable. The blood was taken as always. The drip was started, and pretty soon Dr. Zeiber came walking over carrying the familiar piece of paper. Then she invited my wife, son, and new baby daughter to accompany her into a private room. That was not regular. Not regular at all.

She went on to point out the comparatively large number on that piece of paper. Joshua's white cell count was high. Very high. At first Jana took this as a good sign since white blood cells are the battle cells of the body. She assumed that a high white count meant our little boy was getting healthier. Usually when his white count was high, he had lots of energy and overall felt pretty good. That was correct but only to a point. Dr. Zeiber explained that in the case of leukemia, when the cell count got as high as Joshua's, something was going wrong inside his little body.

The high white count meant that his body was trying to fight something off and trying really hard based on the overly large number. Potentially, Joshua's leukemia was back, and his bone marrow was once again churning out cancerous blood cells that his white cells were trying desperately to fight off. We were sent away from the clinic that day with the word that more tests would be done to see if this was indeed the case.

I met them for lunch at one of those chain, build-your-own burrito restaurants that are the same whether you're in Arkansas or Montana. We walked mindlessly through the line. *Black beans, please, and if you could hold the return of leukemia, that would be great.*

I remember sitting at lunch with my wife and kids, Joshua eating nachos while we stared at our plates with no appetite. Joshua was completely unaware that something out of the new ordinary might be happening inside him; we were internally fighting to hold onto hope that maybe the cancer wasn't back.

In some ways the emotional impact was weightier than when he was initially diagnosed because we now knew what to expect. We knew about the pain and intensity of treatment. We knew about the side effects of relapse and the rigorous cycle of preparation and treatment families seeking a transplant had to go through. The expectation made it worse, and my stomach churned as I began to mull over the possibilities.

I warned myself not to jump to conclusions, to wait for the final results of the further tests they had run, but I couldn't help it. I was thinking down a long line of misery. I was wondering if we had the physical and emotional strength to start over again at day one. I wondered if Joshua had it, too, after coming so far. How do you explain to a little boy that he had to do it all again?

He ate his nachos, and it reminded me of those strips of peanut butter and jelly. Here we were again. A little boy oblivious to the issues of life and death. A father completely powerless to do anything to help his son.

I wanted to believe. God help me, I did. But suddenly I didn't have the luxury of a passive faith anymore. I was realizing again that faith—real faith—is active. And it's hard. Faith is something you have to fight for. It's something you have to choose. And you have to fight and choose in the face of evidence rather than with the evidence on your side.

That lack of evidence or sight is what makes faith faith. By definition, faith is believing something to be real or true even though you can't see it. At least I had the second part of the definition right because I couldn't see Joshua not relapsing. In my mind, he already had, and I was already trying to deal with the fallout.

I tried to tell myself over my rapidly cooling burrito that I needed to have faith, but that's where faith gets problematic, because though we're pretty clear in Christian circles about what faith is, we're not so clear about how to go about having it. I mean, how do you believe? It's a tricky question, right? It's not like making cookies or riding a bike or setting up a Tivo where there is a step-by-step process. You might argue, "There are belief classes! That's what church is!" But most of the time, those classes aren't so much about *how* to believe but *what* to believe. They teach you about doctrine, biblical history, apologetics, or whatever. They teach you what to believe, but they don't teach you how to do it.

In retrospect I think I had subconsciously placed believing and love in the same (albeit incorrect) category—that it's something you just fall into and out of. One day you love someone or something. But the next day you wake up and find that you don't. When someone asks us how to love, you answer the same way you would if someone asked you how to believe: You just do. And that solution works great when you feel like loving. Or you feel like believing. But when you're watching your son who has potentially relapsed into the clutches of cancer lick the nacho cheese off his fingertips while you wait for a phone for a call from the hematologist, it's not quite as helpful. Because in that moment you don't feel like believing.

In that moment what you feel is tired. Hopeless. Despairing. Anxious. Anything but faithful. Good, churchgoing folk would say that you need to "trust the Lord." OK. Easier said than done. At least in that moment.

How discouraging it would have been to have been sitting there with my family, feeling the tension headache start to form behind my eyes, if Jesus Himself had sat down right next to us and said, "Just believe." But Jesus is more realistic than that because there's no "just" to believing. Believing is work.

Work

That's what Jesus said in John 6. Somebody asked Jesus a simple question: "What kind of work do we have to do in order to please God?" Jesus might have responded by saying, "Oh, that's a silly way to ask the question. Faith is the opposite of work. You really don't have to do anything at all; you just believe." Instead He acknowledged the kernel of truth embedded inside the query:

> *"This is the work of God—that you believe in the One He has sent." (John 6:29)*

You don't "just believe." Believing is work. Hard work.

It's simple to say, but up until that point it hadn't really struck me that I had much of a choice in the matter of believing. I was so entrenched in the Christianized world I had formed around myself that such fundamental issues were far from my mind. I was more comfortable discussing the lampstands in Revelation or the finer points of Leviticus than knocking around the issue of choosing to believe. And for the Christian, exercising faith is most definitely a choice.

Initially we are passive parties that are acted upon. Faith is the gift of God that comes to you by His grace and grace alone. But after that point we are armed with the power of the Holy Spirit. The same power that raised Christ from the dead lives inside of us, and the Holy Spirit empowers us to believe. For the Christian, faith is a choice, one we must choose to make in even the seemingly mundane details of life.

Every decision we make, whether good or bad, is deeply rooted in belief. When we are tempted to be greedy with our finances, we have to make a choice to believe that it's better to give than receive. If we believe that's true, we'll act accordingly. If we don't, then we'll build bigger barns to house our stuff. When we are tempted to think that our marriage has grown stale and that we would be more fulfilled outside of it, we have to make a choice to believe that God has placed us together with our spouse. If we don't, then we'll quickly find ourselves on a dating Web site posing as someone younger and cooler than our true selves. When we are tempted to overeat and indulge ourselves, we have to make a choice to believe that our bodies are temples of the Holy Spirit and should be treated as such. If we don't really believe that, then there's all the more reason for an extra piece of pie. And the list goes on and on.

Christianity is about believing, but make no mistake: believing is work. Problem is that many of us are working hard at the wrong thing. We're working hard not to sin. We're working hard to be generous. We're working hard to read the Bible. What we should be working hard to do is believe in each and every one of those situations. We believe that in each of those individual moments, God's resources of grace, power, patience, hope, and endurance won't run dry. We believe in Him as the great supplier of what we need, and we do so one need at a time.

So there we sat, cold burritos and all, and chose to believe. Or at least we tried the best we could to believe. Not to believe that Joshua wasn't relapsing but to believe that God is sovereign. That He is wise. And that's really the core of believing, isn't it? It's not only believing in God's power as much as it is believing in His character.

If all we do is trust God for a positive outcome, we are subtly implying that we, in our own infinite knowledge and wisdom, know what is best. That doesn't mean we don't pray specifically for healing, for an end to suffering, for whatever— we certainly do. But we pray undergirded with confidence not only in what God can do but in who God is. That's really what we are choosing to believe. We are choosing to believe not so much that He would spare us from having to do chemotherapy all over again, but if that is indeed what He chose for us, He would be faithful to uphold us with His strength. Again.

When you're in a situation like that, staring down the barrel of the proverbial gun, you can't help but think about the future. I couldn't imagine having the strength to go through the past year all over again. I couldn't imagine starting over at that point. And the truth is, I didn't have to.

Jesus reminded us to petition God for our *daily* bread. And when we wake up in the morning, to petition Him all over again for tomorrow's bread. The choice to believe is one that must be made over and over again in a myriad of contexts and situations. Sitting there that day, I didn't have to believe about tomorrow. I had to believe for today, and part of believing for today was believing God would help me believe tomorrow all over again. But another part of that belief is recognizing that in this moment—the one right now—I had the choice to believe. And that kind of faith is work. Hard work. But somewhere along the line I had missed the work part of faith.

Believe

Maybe it was a translation issue. The Greeks thought believing exclusively involved the intellect. We have sort of adopted the same idea into our English understanding, that belief is about assenting to a certain set of facts you hold to be true. So the *how* of believing, from that mind-set, involved proof. How you believe is by looking at an empirical set of evidence and then placing your stamp of approval when you see that it demands by logic to be believed. But the Hebrew mind-set is different. In a Hebrew context even the word *believe* takes on a different nuance, one that gets at the suggestion that believing is hard work.

The Hebrew word for *believe* is used all over the Old Testament, but sometimes it takes a little digging to find it. The word appears in Genesis 15:6: "Abram believed the Lord, and He credited it to him as righteousness." This is pretty standard and fits fairly well with our concept of what believing and faith are all about. God told Abraham something, and Abraham took Him at His word. We do the same thing, and we should. God is trustworthy, and our faith in Him is not misplaced. But another usage of the word *believe* in Hebrew is a little more curious.

Exodus 17 is the old Bible story where General Joshua was sent out to fight the Amalekites. Moses presided over the battle, watching it take place below him in the valley. The account goes on to say that the pivotal action in the battle wasn't a matter of strategic military planning or weaponry. The battle ebbed and flowed according to the position of Moses' hands, far above the valley. When Moses held his hands in the air, the Israelites would win the battle. When he lowered them, the tide turned in favor of the Amalekites:

When Moses' hands grew heavy, they took a stone and put it under him, and he sat down on it. Then Aaron and Hur supported his hands, one on one side and one on the other so that his hands remained steady until the sun went down. (Exod. 17:12)

So where's the "belief" in the Exodus passage? The word *believe* is the same as the words translated into English as "remained steady." Now that's interesting and pretty revelatory about the Hebrew concept of belief.

In that understanding, believing isn't something you float in and out of. It's not just about the intellect; it's about perseverance. It's about remaining steady. And it reinforces what I sensed that afternoon—that if I wanted to believe, it wasn't going to be easy. It was going to take work.

How do you believe? You work at it. And sometimes—many times—it's hard work to believe. As hard as holding your hands above your head for an entire day. It's hard to believe God when the circumstances of life are as heavy as your arms at 3:00 p.m. Yet even in this we believe that God will help us believe. We are, in some sense, fighting the battle for belief far below in the valley. And in our story Someone on the hill has His hands in the air. But unlike Moses we are confident that the One on the hill, our Advocate, does not grow tired and weary. Instead, Jesus is continually at the throne of the Father interceding on our behalf, praying for us as we pray for strength in the battle. His hands never go down.

We left our uneaten burritos on the table. Jana took the kids home because it was nap time. Joshua was always exhausted after his trips for treatment. Me? I went back to work. I walked into my office and shut the door. I sat and stared at my computer. Then I stared at the wall. Then I stared at the door. Everything was silent, and I reflected on the fact that life was going on outside my door. Meetings were happening. Faxes were being sent. People were ticking off things on their to-do list one by one. But here, inside my office, time stood still. Quiet and still.

My heart hurt, and I wondered, not for the first time, if you can love someone so much that it was actually painful. And I worked hard to believe. To believe in God's goodness. His wisdom. His grace for this moment in time.

About an hour later, Jana called. Her voice breaking with emotion, she said that our good and faithful doctor and friend had just called her. The cancer was not back. A simple cold was what caused the white blood cell count to be high. God was faithful not only to continue His good work inside Joshua but to uphold us in the moment when believing was so hard. His hands were steady when ours were shaking.

On the subject of belief and faith, we must persevere as the people of God. We must work hard not to do, but to believe.

And in that hard work of believing, we must have the same reaction of Peter that day in John 6. When the crowd was dispersed because of Jesus' radical and controversial teaching, Peter stayed:

> *Lord, who will we go to? You have the words of eternal life. We have come to believe and know that You are the Holy One of God. (John 6:68–69)*

Us too, Peter.

Chapter 11

Redemption

Why?

Before Joshua got sick, I used to spend a good deal of time reflecting about the question *why*. I loved to plumb the depths of the mysteries behind statements, events, and circumstances. I had lengthy discussions about the intricacies of God's sovereignty, the nature of good and evil, and why bad things happen to good people. But at that point I had the luxury of being isolated from those events. In some ways I could sit in judgment of the way other people responded to the pain in their own lives.

I would watch people's reaction to their circumstances and smugly sit back and reflect about the sovereignty of God. Clearly, at least in my mind, these people had never bothered to think about the *why*. And by the *why*, I didn't mean the "woe as me" kind of why. I meant that those people were not pausing to reflect on what God might be up to in their situations. That He wasn't absent but working toward a greater good. That He was teaching them things.

Those people were too caught up in their own pain, tears, and misery to remember that God is always in control. They didn't seem to get it; clearly they weren't able to zoom back with a wide-angle view and look at the big picture. I told myself that if I ever suffered, I would make myself think deeply about it. I told myself I would pensively reflect and learn great spiritual truths in the midst of my pain. I would see my own hardship as a tremendous opportunity to know the deepest parts of spirituality.

That's what I used to think.

Then we found ourselves with the proverbial shoe on the other foot, and suddenly I turned around and two years had gone by since Joshua's diagnosis. And I realized that despite all my spiritual posturing and theoretical idealizing, I had spent the bulk of those twenty-four months just trying to make it through. I didn't spend a lot of time thinking. Or postulating. Or observing.

Several times during those two years, I tried to start a journal so I could record my thoughts and feelings. And there were even a few times when well-meaning people told us, "God must be teaching you so much through this process." I could never keep up the habit of writing, though, much as I wanted to. I wasn't trying to learn lessons; in the end I was just trying to get through the best I could.

Often I think that's the case. Much as we might want to be learners from God in the classroom of pain, only when we get a little distance from the period of intense suffering do we actually have time to look back on and see all He might have been doing in and through us during those moments of hardship.

But once we do have that distance, when things have cooled off a little bit, we can look back and finally ask, "Why?" It's not that I thought God was using my son as some sort of object lesson to me; that wasn't it at all. It was more the sense that, whether we knew it or not, the Lord was using cancer to break up unplowed ground in my heart.

After two years of pills, hospitalizations, pregnancy, and job change, and despite my best attempts to medicate and isolate myself, I found that indeed the Lord had been at work inside me.

I saw glimpses of patience, faith, and perseverance that had risen up through the gracious work of God. These character traits had been forged through the crushing of pills, shaving of heads, and changing of diapers. Like someone who turns around one day and can't believe he's sixty years old, we suddenly began to see many of the things God had done, even (and maybe especially) when we thought He was absent.

Time brought the luxury of reflection on the past, and while we were able to see in that reflection the hand of God at work in and through us, we also began to be acutely aware of some of the things lacking in Joshua. And in us. I guess that's the other side of reflection. You don't just see the good that has come out of your pain; you also begin to see just how much you have lost. Interestingly enough, this reflection hit a high point in the most unlikely of places—on the baseball field.

Baseball

Even though Joshua was at that time a cancer patient, he was also a five-year-old. And so we wanted to let him be a part of stuff that other five-year-olds were doing. So we signed him up for baseball.

Jana and I both played sports all the way through high school, and we wanted our kids to learn to appreciate them as well. But from the beginning, our venture into sporting events for five-year-olds seemed doomed to fail. Because of a misplaced *e* on an e-mail list, we missed the first couple of practices, and when we finally made it, it was a Saturday after Joshua's big treatment. Only a few days earlier he was shot full of chemotherapy from both his port and through a spinal tap. He was already feeling crummy, but there he was—excited to be wearing his new pants and holding his new bat, trying to figure out which hand his glove went on. Joshua had little experience with baseball because while other kids had been learning the finer points of fielding grounders, he had been in bed. I reasoned, though, that this would take care of itself because, after all, this was a four-, five-, and six-year-old league. How competitive could it really be?

When I first started playing baseball, we hit the ball off a tee. If you hit it out of the infield, you were virtually assured of getting a home run. All the kids ran around bumping into one another for an hour or so, then everybody sat down and had a Coke. After the season you pretty much forgot about baseball until the next year when all the teams were divided up again and you started relearning the game. It was like taking two steps forward and one step back.

Apparently things had changed.

Joshua jumped out of the car to his first practice and waddled out onto the field, the way he always did after a chemo treatment. The medicine always made him retain water and limp due to the leg pain, which made physical activity awkward at best. And to my horror, I looked around to see no tees. And that's not all.

The kids were taking infield. And throwing to first base. *And catching the ball!* I had to check myself to remember that these kids were indeed Joshua's age. For the next two hours

I watched these regular kids from the neighborhood do things Joshua was completely incapable of doing. They caught pop flies. They fielded ground balls. And our little boy tottered around trying to remember which was first base and which was third. By the end of practice, Joshua could hardly stand. Unfortunately for him, he still had base-running drills to do.

Joshua straggled in to home plate, his only consolation that I had a Gatorade waiting for him after practice. The kids were to line up at home plate, and the coach was going to send them around the bases at half-second intervals. The kid who was able to pass the most other players while running would win. The coach strategically placed the kids in order of their speed, and Joshua found his place last in line. Then it started.

"Go. Go. Go. Go." One at a time they tore out, and I was amazed to see how smoothly they ran. How their energy seemed to be limitless. How they were able to laugh and yell without concentrating on every step.

"Go. Go. Go."

A sense of dread started to come on me as a dad. It was the same feeling that had made the last two hours an excruciatingly long experience. I felt like at any moment Joshua's world—the one we had carefully constructed and guarded him in for the past two years—would come crashing down. I imagined crowds of children pointing and laughing at him because he ran awkwardly. Or because he couldn't run at all. Or because his belly was bigger than theirs. Or because his cheeks were puffy.

"Go. Go. Go."

And then I imagined that none of those things might happen. Sure, he would be slow, but maybe he could at least make it around the bases. Maybe he could dig deeply from some reservoir of strength that he should not have and actually make it. Maybe he could do it after all. Maybe. So I began to pray one of those desperation type prayers—you know the kind—where you feel that the fate of the world depends on whether or not your son actually crosses home plate still standing. The words started slipping out my mouth involuntarily: "Please, Jesus, please . . ."

"Go."

He took off, and he tried. He tried so hard. His arms and legs flailed in most every direction. It was barely faster than a walk, but he tried. At least he did for about ten yards, then he stopped. He considered. Then he took a shortcut across the infield in a burst of blazing speed, hit third base, and turned for home. He finished in front of everyone and threw up his hands in triumph, boldly declaring, "I passed everybody!" And everything seemed fine for a second. I realized I had stopped breathing and exhaled mightily. My heart was in my throat, and tears were in my eyes, and I started to think, "Hey—a funny moment. It's going to be OK." But you know how understanding kids are about stuff like that.

The calls started from the other boys: "He cheated!"

"That's not fair!"

"He didn't touch all the bases!"

The coach was quick to jump to Joshua's defense, explaining that Joshua had never played baseball before, and slowly the crowd disbanded, and everyone went their separate ways.

Joshua straggled over to me, half of his shirttail hanging out. On the one hand, I wanted to wrap my arms around him and kiss and hug him and tell him that I was so proud of him because I knew it was hard and that he tried his best and that he was my boy and I loved him so much. The other part of me wanted to climb to the top of the stands and scream at everyone there, "Do you know how many needles this five-year-old has been stuck with? You have no idea how much pain he is in, so if he doesn't want to touch all the bases that's just fine!" I wanted to announce his cancer with a bullhorn and trumpet it as an excuse for his awkward gate and misunderstanding of the finer points of base running.

But instead we walked with our heads down to the dugout. I picked up his little glove, the one we had just bought for him and that hadn't even been used before this practice. It was stiff from lack of use. I picked up his T-ball bat, and it felt as small as a toothpick in my hands. I put these things in his bat bag and threw it over my shoulder. Then we limped slowly back to the car in an awkward silence. It seemed like a lot longer than fifty or sixty yards, with his little cleats clicking on the sidewalk.

I could hear the uneven pace of his pained legs in those steps. Finally Joshua spoke.

"Daddy?"

"Yes, son."

"I'm the worst baseball player ever."

And the dam broke. Tears flooded his eyes. And they flooded mine too. I knew that there was nothing I could possibly say to make up for the disappointment of the moment. He wanted to be good so badly, and yet it was physically impossible for him. I didn't know what to say, so I grabbed my son and held him tightly. Maybe too tightly. My heart burned in my chest like it was going to rupture. But rupture with what? With love? No doubt. With pity? Absolutely—for him and for myself. But there was something else there, too.

In that moment I was not pensive. I didn't reflect on everything the Lord had taught us through the past couple of years. Instead, I felt an overwhelming sense of loss. Loss of innocence for me and for Joshua. Loss of the simple pleasure of hitting a baseball and being good at it. Loss of the enjoyment of little moments. It was devastating, probably more for me than for him.

I suppose that's normal, but it's weird how that sense of loss overtakes you at the most unexpected times. You feel like you have regained a sense of equilibrium, that life is a bit more normal, and then you go to baseball practice. Or the holidays roll around. Or you hear a song. Or you smell a smell. And suddenly, in that moment when you least expect it, you are overcome with how radically different life really is. And how much you have indeed lost.

That's not to say we didn't appreciate and recognize all we had gained over the past two years. Patience. Hope. A new understanding of what it meant to love and be loved, and a new appreciation of the everyday moments of life. But the sweetness of the gain was tempered with the bitterness of loss.

I started the car and drove home. Eventually the tears dried up. And if you asked Joshua two weeks later about his first baseball practice, it's doubtful he would care to remember much about it at all. But I would. I do. Not just because of how acute the emotions were that day but because through that experience I began to learn about the true nature of redemption.

Redemption

Up to that day on the baseball field, I thought I understood something about redemption. I knew, for example, that the word literally means "to buy back." I had preached sermons about redemption, mainly focusing on how redemption is different in the Bible from in the modern world.

I would wax eloquently about the way our culture assumes redemption is something an individual should pursue. For example, if a guy spent his teenage years selling drugs on the streets, he should spend a good chunk in the second half of his life working to take drugs off the street. Redemption, in this sense, is something that can and should be achieved. You are meant to atone for your cultural sins by doing a better job as a human and helping out your fellow humans. We were the source of problems, and we've got to do something to work ourselves out of it.

The spirit of self-justification lives deeply within all our hearts.

But when the Bible talks about "redemption," certain images would have immediately come into the minds of its ancient readers. For the Greek the word referred to a large price slaves might save up to buy their own freedom. This was possible since slaves during this time were occasionally paid, and many times someone could save up over time enough to buy his way out. For the Jewish reader the word would take him back to the Old Testament. In that context the word was used not only to describe the price paid to free a slave but also to represent some of God's great acts of the past.

The Exodus, for example, when the Israelites were brought up out of slavery in Egypt was described in this way. Both images point to one of the key truths about redemption—that there is always a price to be paid. And it's expensive.

Make no mistake, in God's economy redemption does have a cost, but it's not a cost we pay. In God's economy He pays the price for redemption. Jesus is our redemption, and by Him we are brought out of slavery. Out of sin. Out of death. A finality and a totality are associated with redemption; in a salvific sense we have been redeemed by the precious blood of Christ. The price has been paid, and we will live forever as the children of God.

Yep, I knew something about redemption but not as much as I thought. I only saw the gain—we were once slaves; now we are free. We were once imprisoned to sin and death; now we are children of God. Jesus has redeemed us from all of this, but redemption goes beyond the realm of heaven and hell.

In real life, though, an aspect of redemption isn't so cheery.

God was buying back our experience with cancer, and the results were obvious. He was healing Joshua physically, and He was working good in our lives as well. We were becoming more like Christ. But that process was one of great pain and great loss. In redeeming our circumstances, God doesn't promise, nor does He try, to make up for the stuff that happens in our lives as if He owed us some good for allowing some bad. He's not into paybacks like that.

God's not too concerned about tipping the scales in our lives, making sure that because we are "Christians" our positive life experiences outweigh the negative ones. There will never be a moment when we will stand on top of our circumstances and say, "Yes. Now it's finally evened out." It just doesn't work like that.

I don't think it worked like that for someone like Joseph, though he knew much about both losing and gaining. Betrayed and sold into slavery by his brothers, remaining faithful to the Lord, despite being falsely imprisoned and moving in and out of positions of lowliness as well as loftiness, Joseph knew something about loss and gain. Sure, he did have that one great moment at the end of the story. You remember the one—the scene is the throne room of Egypt. He had been in charge of the empire for some time and had made plans to care for the people during the famine he knew was coming. And lo and behold, who should walk into the throne room but his treacherous brothers—the same ones who had sold him into slavery all those years earlier. They didn't recognize Joseph; they had come there to beg for food because they were starving. Then there was the big revelation when he told them just who he was. Some might argue that in the throne room that day redemption finally happened. Joseph got back more than he lost. But that doesn't seem like redemption to me; it seems like vindication.

Nor does redemption really seem like the appropriate word for the tragic story of Job. Job—who lost his children, his wife, his possessions, and even his health—was given those things and more back at the end of his life. But I doubt in that moment Job was ready to pump his fits and shout, "Redemption!" because he was richer than he was before God and Satan made their bet.

No, God's definition of redemption doesn't involve evening out prosperity or supposed blessings. And it sure doesn't seem like it involves a lot of giddy smiles and trite reflections on what we have lost, as if to say, "Boy, it's all been worth it." Redemption is about both gain and loss. That's what I was feeling sitting on the cold, metal stands of the baseball park. And I took great comfort in knowing that in this, as in all cases, the Bible is honest if we care to actually look deeply into it. I tried to do just that, to find something in those pages that articulated what I was feeling. Something that either validated or corrected my sense of both gain and loss. And I found a prophet who knew the great joy of the coming Messiah and the searing pain of a home in shambles.

Jeremiah

Jeremiah wasn't called the weeping prophet for nothing. Here was the man God chose to be His mouthpiece to an entire society. The problem was that nobody was listening. Time and time again Jeremiah warned his countrymen of the impending judgment of God. He tried to tell them that God was going to do the unthinkable—rip their country and heritage out from under them by raising up a pagan people to come and deport them. For that message Jeremiah was put in the stocks. He was ridiculed. His scrolls were burned.

When we pick up the narrative in Jeremiah 32, Jerusalem was under siege for a second time. Jeremiah was under house arrest, confined in the city by a royal guard. There was a brief break in the action as the besieging army of Babylon withdrew to face an Egyptian force marching toward Palestine. During that time Jeremiah was visited by his cousin, Hanamel, and a transaction occurred.

Much of an Israelite family's identity was tied to its possessions, especially its property. So important was the land that it could not be sold outside the clan. During difficult times, however, the property could be used as collateral and sold to members within the family. This was Hanamel's proposition to his cousin Jeremiah.

Evidently Hanamel needed money for food or to pay some debt, and the only thing he had left was the land. Now I don't know about you, but I can't think of a worse time to be thinking about buying and selling land than when your city is under siege from a hostile force. After all, the writing was on the wall; the Babylonians were going to outlast the Israelites. They would be deported. They were going to lose their land, maybe permanently. And here comes Cousin Hanamel with a real estate deal. Seems like some ocean-front property in Arizona to me.

But Jeremiah bought the land. Literally, he "redeemed" the land (Jer. 32:8). Can you imagine what the people around him were saying? "Sucker. Moron. Fool. Doesn't he see what's happening all around us?" And yet Jeremiah bought. At one of the darkest moments in the history of God's chosen people, when the siege was ongoing and the fall of Jerusalem was just a matter of time, Jeremiah bought some property because "houses, fields, and vineyards will again be bought in this land" (Jer. 32:15).

Jeremiah redeemed the land in the middle of tragedy. This wasn't a moment of great triumph. It certainly wasn't an evening out of circumstances. But then again, that's not how redemption works.

Redemption isn't about forgetting. It's not even about the question of whether or not everything that's happened has been "worth it." Redemption is about faith. It's about trusting that God can and will do all He says He can and will do. And here's what He told Jeremiah He was doing:

> "I will surely gather them from all the lands where I banish them in my furious anger and great wrath; I will bring them back to this place and let them live in safety. They will be my people, and I will be their God. I will give them singleness of heart and action, so that they will always fear me for their own good and the good of their children after them. I will make an everlasting covenant

with them: I will never stop doing good to them, and I will inspire them to fear me, so that they will never turn away from me. I will rejoice in doing them good and will assuredly plant them in this land with all my heart and soul."

"This is what the LORD says: As I have brought all this great calamity on this people, so I will give them all the prosperity I have promised them. Once more fields will be bought in this land of which you say, 'It is a desolate waste, without men or animals, for it has been handed over to the Babylonians.'" (Jer. 32:37–38)

That's the key. The land itself is the symbol of redemption. God wasn't going to give them a new land; He's going to work on the land that's been bought. He's not taking them somewhere different. He's returning them to the same hills that once lay desolate. Out of that desolation He will bring prosperity.

New

Redemption doesn't mean you stand in triumph over your circumstances. And it doesn't mean that the "new" makes you forget about everything that happened in the "old" (although in heaven someday these light and momentary afflictions will pale in comparison). Redemption is about the confidence that God is bringing good out of the bad, prosperity out of desolation. God's not interested in evening things out; He's interested in taking those things which are so painful, earth-shattering, and devastating and turning them into marks of His goodness and kindness.

Moses was a shepherd for forty years, but God redeemed his experience in the desert. He gained a knowledge of the land that would be vital because he spent the next forty years leading the children of Israel through the same desert. David spent his childhood learning how to defend sheep with meager weapons. God redeemed his defensive skills as he shepherded the people of Israel, slaying giants with small stones. Luke had an obsessively ordered and detailed mind, but God redeemed it, enabling him to record in a logical way the ministry of Christ and the early church. Paul spent years studying and memorizing the Torah, and God redeemed that knowledge as he became an apologist in the midst of Jews and Gentiles alike.

We often think God is in the business of swooping down and plucking us out of our circumstances. He rescues us to be sure—from sin and death and hopelessness. But His rescue incorporates those sad, tragic, devastating circumstances we want, in the moment, to see removed. In redemption God takes the shattered blocks of our lives and slowly, methodically, but faithfully, puts them back together in a way we couldn't have imagined at first. In the end there is something new and different, and yet it's made up of those same pieces of life that once looked so broken on the ground.

Joshua's baseball season got a little better but not much. I wish I could say that by the end of the year he was popping home runs or running seamlessly around the bases. Or I wish I could say that the entire team and all their immediate relatives became Christians just from being around us. None of that happened. But that doesn't mean this seemingly small part of our story wasn't, and won't, continue to be redeemed. Perhaps that's what's happening right now, as I finish typing this paragraph.

The refrain echoes through Joseph's elevator-like life: "You planned evil against me; God planned it for good" (Gen. 50:20). That's what we are confident of when we believe in redemption. We are confident that God is always at work, in big and small ways. He's working inside of cancer. Inside job loss. Inside suffering of all kinds. God is at work, constantly redeeming. He's taking the crumbling remnants of our lives and putting them back together.

And how do we respond to the knowledge of His redemption? We buy land. We play baseball. We write books. We continue to live and hope and believe, and that belief works itself in these tangible ways. We say with our actions that we may be confused during these circumstances, but we nonetheless remain confident that God is with us. He is for us. And that's why we're buying this field.

Chapter 12

Wisdom

Make-A-Wish

I love the Make-A-Wish Foundation®. It's one thing to see the TV ads and the promotional bumper stickers; it's another thing to be a recipient of the generosity of others. The foundation's mission statement is this: "We grant the wishes of children with life-threatening medical conditions to enrich the human experience with hope, strength and joy." And that's what they do every single day.

A quick conversation with a Wish rep or a casual stroll through their Web site reveals literally thousands of wishes that have been granted. You read stories of kids meeting their football and baseball heroes and sitting on the bench with them in the dugout. You hear of girls going on shopping sprees and having their bedrooms made over. And you see these heartbreakingly beautiful pictures of children with bald heads and puffy cheeks that fade into the background because of their brilliant smiles as they sit with their heroes, travel to their dream destinations, or experience thrills of a lifetime.

As we drew close to the end of Joshua's treatment cycle, we were approached by a Wish representative asking us what his wish might be. We sat at our kitchen table for the Wish interview—basically a conversation to make sure that we as parents weren't influencing our son to wish for our mortgage to be paid off or for a new computer or something like that. The interview with Jacilyn, the Wish coordinator, had some rough spots but was indeed revelatory:

Jacilyn: What's your favorite food?

Joshua: Strawberries

(Wow—pretty healthy start Joshua. Maybe you should have said prime rib.)

Jacilyn: How about junk food? Do you like chips, or candy?

Joshua: Yes. I like Sun Chips.

(Hmmm . . . we've had Sun Chips once. At lunch yesterday. Daddy likes Skittles, Joshua.)

Jacilyn: What if you could have anything in the world? What would you want?

Joshua: A Wall-E movie.

(What? Really? How about a life-sized robot to cook and clean instead? Or maybe a Hummer?)

Jacilyn: If you could meet anybody in the world, who would it be? Like a football player or a baseball player?

Joshua: Eli. I would meet Eli.

(That's great. Your cousin Eli. That you see three times a week.)

There wasn't a lot to draw from in that conversation, so it was left mainly to us as parents to provide guidance for the wish. We went with the old standby, that great granter of wishes for kids of all ages—Disney World. So the trip was planned, the details were worked out, and we were excited.

Disney

After several months the week of Joshua's Orlando-themed wish rolled around. Promptly at 7:00 a.m., a white stretch limousine rolled into our driveway to take us to the airport. Joshua couldn't believe that there was orange juice in the car, which he properly drank out of a champagne flute during the ride. We were blown away from the start at the level of generosity and care from the organization, and it just got better when we landed in Orlando. Evidently Disney and the Make-A-Wish Foundation® work together so often to grant so many wishes that there is an entire complex in Orlando just for Wish families. It's called the "Give Kids the World Village," and it's pretty fantastic.

Each family has their own villa with two or three bedrooms, kitchen, and washer and dryer. There is an ice cream parlor that opens at 7:00 a.m. every morning. You can pick up the phone twenty-four hours a day and order pizza. Volunteers work the on-site restaurant, serving you from the moment you walk in the door. There's a castle with a merry-go-round. There's a fishing pond, two swimming pools, a movie theater, and an arcade. Disney and comic-book characters come to visit every day, and every night there is a different themed party. I thought Joshua's head was going to explode.

And that's not to mention the actual parks of Orlando. We were given tickets to all the Disney Parks and Universal Studios. In addition we had this handy-dandy lanyard that held a "special assistance" badge. That badge gave us a free pass to the front of every line, whether we wanted to ride Splash Mountain or meet Cinderella. And we used it liberally.

Day 1 was spent at the Magic Kingdom. Now, we were all a little nervous at this point because for as long as I can remember, Joshua has hated two things in equal measure: squash and people dressed in costumes. Both terrify him. But much to our great amazement and amusement, there he was at the Magic Kingdom, hugging Pluto and giving Donald Duck a high five. The day couldn't have gone better, and we returned to the village exhausted. Joshua, though, dug deep and found the energy and strength so he could be outside for the nightly parade down the streets of Give Kids the World.

Day 2 was Animal Kingdom. We started the day at Donald's Safari Breakfast, eating with Mickey, Minnie, and the Duck himself. Several doughnuts and bowls of sugar-based cereal later, we were off to tackle the wildlife. Another grand day ensued, and we relaxed over dinner as the retiree volunteers served Joshua bowl after bowl of ice cream. But the best was yet to come.

Sea World

Sea World was Joshua's only real solid point of identification for the trip. We had looked at Disney books, watched Disney movies, and visited the Disney World Web site, but the whole concept of a Disney park remained ethereal to his five-year-old mind. Sea World, on the other hand, was something he could grab onto.

When he was about eighteen months old, we went to Sea World in San Antonio, and Joshua talked frequently about it for the next three years. Sea World was what he remembered, and he remembered it to be absolutely awesome. So when his wish was granted, he was most excited about going back there. That was the destination for day 3. When we put Joshua in bed after his day at Animal Kingdom, he was wide-eyed and excited. He couldn't wait for morning. On the other hand, Jana and I were exhausted, secretly wondering if we had the stamina to keep up with our cancer-stricken son.

He went to bed about 8:30, and we sat in the living room planning the next day. It was about 10:00 when we heard coughing coming from the back room. I remember that it was soft but distinct—with a barking-like quality. So after a few minutes of the insistent sound, Jana got up to check the situation. What we found in the back room brought us crashing back to reality.

There was our son—the little boy who had endured so much over the past three years, the one who had bravely taken so many needles, chewed so many pills, and fought so hard— sitting upright in his bed. He was clutching his new Mickey Mouse to his chest, covering up his mouth so that his coughs would be quiet. His face was red from crying. Joshua knew this drill. He'd been through it before. And by this time he knew his body pretty well. All he said, between his fits of coughing, was, "Can we still go to Sea World?"

As I've earlier described, in the world of leukemia, when a kid gets a fever, it disrupts life. The fever threshold is 100.5. Beyond that, we have to go to the emergency room because something's going on inside him. And even a normal infection might potentially be concerning because of a depressed immune system due to chemotherapy.

Before that night it had been over five months since we had gone to the emergency room. And leading up to that trip, we enlisted everyone we knew to pray for us, that we would be able to stay healthy for the duration of our time down south.

Joshua knew he was sick, and the thermometer proved it: 102.7. We jumped in the car and headed to downtown Orlando to the children's hospital. Even though by the time we got there Joshua was singing songs and feeling fine, his temperature was still up, and his blood counts proved to be low. They were lower in fact than they had been in months, meaning that the docs at the ER checked us into a room upstairs.

No Sea World. Vacation over.

In all the hurry of finding directions to the hospital and getting there, I hadn't really had time to process everything going on inside me. But as I left Jana and Joshua there at the hospital at about 3:00 a.m., my emotional state went from sadness to anger pretty quickly. I had a solid forty-five-minute car ride back to Give Kids the World to pick up our freshly unpacked bags to take back to the hospital and plenty of time to brood. Suddenly all those feelings and emotions I thought I had processed came rushing back to the surface. The wound, the brokenness, and the loss of the last three years felt fresh. I felt like I was emotionally bleeding, having been stabbed once again by cancer. And I said some things to the Lord I'm not proud of:

"Why now? What are You doing? Can't we get a break?"

"Would it really disrupt the eternal plan of the universe for this little boy to get to go to Sea World?"

"I'm sick of learning things. I'm tired of my life being an object lesson. I want a week off."

That last one really seemed to fit. I was tired. Sick and tired. I didn't want to learn any more. I didn't want to grow any more. And the thought of my sick son being a faith object lesson was enough to make me wretch. I wanted to go to Sea World for both of us.

And didn't we deserve it? I certainly thought so, if I'm being honest. I mean, sure, I'm as self-medicating as the next guy. But we did our best. We tried hard. We tried to remain positive and continue to seek the Lord. Was going to see Shamu jump through some hoops really too much to ask?

That's the thought I carried with me through the rest of the night and early the next morning. Like a metronome of self-justification, I kept hearing, "We deserve this. We deserve this. We deserve this." I guess that's the reset mode for most of us.

Whenever we're backed into a corner, we tend to drop either consciously or subconsciously into self-justification. We want to prove how right, deserving, smart, creative, or, ironically, secure we are. We justify our fear, failure, arrogance, pride, and doubt. But in the end all of these efforts at self-justification are really just a façade because we know, way down deep, that we don't want what we deserve. If we really got what we deserved, we would all be in a heap of trouble. So we justify, talking ourselves into believing that we deserve something else than what we're getting.

Into this carefully crafted construct steps the gospel, which is based squarely on the principle that we cannot justify ourselves. We have no excuse. That is precisely the reason we need Christ to do the justifying for us. The gospel forces us to look our absolute inability square in the eye and to do so over and over again.

These are things we know as Christians. We know we don't deserve better. We know we can't expect better. We know we all deserve much, much worse; but in the moment we want to go to Sea World. We don't want to be sick anymore. We're tired of being poor. We're tired of struggling. So even though we might know good and well the insanity of our self-justification, we can't help ourselves. It's a battle all the way back, but fortunately it's a battle Jesus is willing to fight for us. That's what happened later that day.

Repent

We settled into our small room, wondering if indeed our vacation was over—a disappointed little boy and a really angry dad. But time is a helpful ally to Jesus. With time comes perspective; and after a night in the ER and half a day in the hospital,

I had the chance to cool off. We did, after all, have two really great days. Most people don't even get that. Joshua's overall prognosis was good. And he even seemed to have somewhat forgotten about Sea World (we sure weren't bringing it up). I began thinking that perhaps I had overreacted, and I began to hear the same still, small voice inside me reminding me that I had some things to be sorry for.

Where to begin that list? It's certainly long and undistin-guished, but there was something I genuinely felt I needed to apologize to the Lord for. It wasn't the anger. I think God can take that; His chest is big enough for me to pound. And I'm certainly not the first person to express anger to God. You don't have to turn far in the book of Psalms to find worse than what I said. No, I didn't think I needed to be sorry for being mad. I did, however, feel that my attitude had called the wisdom of God into question. That's what I needed to apologize for. But apologizing doesn't really take it far enough. God doesn't only call for apologies and confession; He calls for repentance.

To *repent* means "to turn." That's what God wanted from me. He didn't just want me to stop being angry. Nor did He only want an apology. He wanted me to turn. To switch directions. To stop doubting and to start trusting. To stop complaining and start giving thanks. Repentance is not just stopping but turning and walking in the opposite direction.

Specifically, in this context, I needed to repent of questioning the wisdom of God in allowing our vacation to be interrupted. In that repentance I needed to turn instead in faith, believing that God does indeed know what He is doing. And what He is doing is good, even if I can't see how. Repentance in this situation meant acknowledging my tremendous lack of vision and radical inability to appreciate the grand nature of God's bigger plan and purpose. It meant turning from the idea that I somehow knew better than He how our lives should be turning out.

Isn't that what we do when we complain about our circumstances? We assume that we have a better idea of how the world should be run. That we are wiser than the Lord. That our plans are better than His.

But let's be serious. Where would we be if we ran the world?

So the best way I knew how, I prayed with Jana and repented of my arrogance and pride and tried as best I could to express our choice to try and trust the wisdom of God. I didn't expect anything in return. I'd moved past the hope that God would reveal the mysteries behind His decision. I think that's how it should be. When I repented of questioning the wisdom of God, I assumed that for one reason or another it was important that we not go to Sea World. Maybe it's because a bomb would go off there. Maybe it's because we would get in a car wreck. We never know.

The vast majority of the time, you simply have to trust that there is reason behind it. You choose to believe that God is not just with you but that God is for you.

For

I suppose sitting in that hospital room, with my wife's hands in mine, it shouldn't have been so difficult to believe that God was "for" us. He'd certainly demonstrated His commitment to our good over the past years.

When our son got sick and we needed financial provision, God proved His "for-ness." When I was battling depression and purpose in life, God proved His "for-ness." When I didn't know how to lead my family and what direction to take them, God proved His "for-ness." And even in the life of my son who, though he didn't know the full extent of it, was engaged in a battle for his very life, God had proved His "for-ness."

God had moved us to a town with an incredible children's hospital. He'd given me a job that provided for our family. He'd given us friends and family that had sacrificed for our well-being. And if we still doubted, there was the historically proven fact of His for-ness.

We need look no further than the hillside at Calvary to know that God is not just with us but for us.

But me? Well, I wanted my son to go to Sea World. But by God's grace we began to pray in that hospital room. We reminded ourselves of the proven faithfulness of God in Jesus Christ. As best as we knew how, we turned and trusted in the wisdom of His will.

In so much as we were able, we once again affirmed that we believed He was working for our good through hardship and difficulty. He was working for our good through suffering. He was working for our good through pain. He was working for our good through missing Sea World and spending time in the Arnold Palmer Children's Hospital in Orlando, Florida. For the life of me, I couldn't see how, but faith does not require understanding. It helps, sure—but knowledge of exactly what God is up to in a single moment is not a prerequisite for believing that He is indeed up to something. Even if we don't know what that something is.

That's how it happens most of the time when you meet with disappointment. You accept that two levels of reality are happening at the same time, though you rarely (if ever) get the chance for the door of heaven to be cracked enough to peer inside.

Inside

Meanwhile, the doctors told us that we were likely to be released soon to go back to our vacation. It was great news, and we attributed it to all the people praying for us back home. And then God cracked the door.

We were sitting in the playroom at the hospital, and we struck up a conversation with another family. They were from the Detroit area, have four kids, and were at the beach on their family vacation. They had chosen to come to the beach despite the fact that the father worked in the auto industry and his job was recently lost through downsizing. But they had the vacation on the books, and even though they would probably soon be moving if he could find another job, they wanted to enjoy some time in Florida anyway. Their youngest son started acting strangely on their vacation, and they found themselves at the Orlando Children's Hospital.

That's when their two-year-old was diagnosed with leukemia.

On their vacation.

With three siblings still at the beach, unaware of what was truly afflicting their younger brother.

Can you imagine? Strange city, strange people, strange disease—and yet here we were, randomly, together in the same room.

We had a lot to talk about. They were able to ask questions and get honest answers about the treatment. We were able to laugh and cry together. But most importantly, they were able to see Joshua. I noticed how intently they watched him, with his full head of hair, bouncing off the walls like nothing was at all wrong. Here was a kid, three years after the fact, who had been diagnosed with the exact kind of leukemia as their son at the exact age of their son. And he looked to be just fine.

Very coincidental, don't you think?

It was as if God had flipped the switch on Joshua's fever and divinely appointed that moment. And then it was done. As quickly as it had come, Joshua's fever was gone, his counts rebounded remarkably quickly, and we were released after thirty-six hours in the hospital, able to go and do everything we wanted on the trip. The Foundation extended our stay. We went to Sea World after all. Shamu jumped through a hoop. Joshua and I sat in the splash zone. We got wet and ate nachos. But we did so with a profound appreciation for the fact that we were part of something bigger.

Few moments in life are like that. Moments where you see the intricate hand of God, skillfully weaving together misfortune and hope, laughter and tears. It was a moment where we saw things coming together in a new and fresh way, and it was incredibly humbling. Another reminder that we are loved by a busy God. He's a God constantly working and moving in ways we cannot understand and fathom, working for the good of all who love Him. He does right. He does what is best. Always.

God doesn't promise or often deliver a glimpse behind the scenes. But every so often, we get a taste. And all we can do is sit back and marvel at our God. At our wise, wise God.

Chapter 13

Peace

End

Time marches on. Boy, that's a cliché. But who can argue with truth? Time does indeed march; sometimes you feel as though the footsteps are through quicksand, that each step is an arduous effort and the seconds pass by agonizingly slow. But then again it does feel like you turn around one day and you're going to your high school reunion. Or a kid is going to kindergarten. Or college. The march goes on.

In the winter of 2009, we stood and marveled that Joshua was on the verge of finishing chemotherapy. After more than one hundred chemotherapy treatments, somewhere in the neighborhood of three thousand pills, and 1,156 days, just like that, it was going to be done.

I remember when Joshua was first diagnosed: we were sitting in the clinic, Jana pregnant with our second child, and Joshua just starting to lose his hair. Our world was crashing in around us. Our eyes were perpetually red from tears in those days, and every time a doctor approached my heart would start beating faster. Neither of us slept much. We came to the hospital with the dazed look of accident victims, not really keeping track of the hours, days, or weeks.

We sat there trying to figure out life when a bubbly mother and son proudly marched in, and because of the shout that went up, we learned that he was there for his last appointment. *His last appointment.* We looked longingly at the impromptu celebration taking place in front of us, then we looked at each other. We didn't have to say it; each of us knew what the other was thinking. *We would never be that family.* Not us. It was too far away—a vision of a distant future that was much in doubt. Maybe we would never be happy and carefree like that again.

And then, just like that, we were that family.

We were the ones who were graduating from this period. We were the ones saying good-bye and hello at the same time. We were the ones with the doctors and nurses slapping high fives and breaking out in spontaneous tears and applause. And our son—*our son*—was the one with the full head of hair and smile that was both enormous and shy at the same time. *We were the ones who finished.* And in the days and weeks leading up to the December 20 mark, the day of the last pill, there was time to reflect. Like climbers just a few feet from the top, we turned around and surveyed everything that was left in the wake. There was loss. There was gain. There were relationships that had shattered on the rocks below, and there were others who were proudly standing beside us. But there was something else, too.

At least for me, there was a sense of conflict. That conflict, I think, came for a number of reasons. Maybe it's not that dissimilar to what someone finally emerging from an alcoholic haze might feel, but in a weird way I was nervous about life without leukemia. For the past three and a half years, much as I might have denied it to be the case, a good chunk of my family's identity had been defined by this illness. And I for one had grown used to that distinction. It was awful to be sure, but it was also part of our family's story that made us unique. In some ways I was nervous about moving forward, wondering exactly who we would be as a family apart from this.

I don't think I'm unique in that. Many people grow so comfortable with their ailments and their struggles that they become defined by that bottle in their hand, the one they love and hate at the same time. To have it stripped away provides an enormous sense of freedom and release and yet at the same time leaves a huge gap. Of course, with cancer as well as rehabilitation from addiction, you move forward in faith, trusting that your identity is firmly seated in Christ. You don't need that other stuff to tell you who you are. Jesus does a fine job on His own.

But there was another reason I had a sense of anxiety about the future, and this one was more practical. I didn't know if Joshua's cancer would come back. I think it was hard for many people, with good reason, to understand this mixed emotion. It certainly would seem like there would be no room for anything except celebration for a child finishing a long series of cancer treatments and having the doctors smiling and slapping high fives at the end of it. But I couldn't help myself.

I had official answers to give those who asked how we felt to be coming to such a significant milestone: "It feels great. What a sense of relief! Yes, we couldn't be happier. Yep, his prognosis is good and we have every reason to be hopeful for the future." But underneath was the nonofficial version of the story, one that was shared only with select people who looked at me with doubt in their eyes when they got the official version: "No, the journey isn't over. There's still the danger of relapse, and I'm not sure we could do this all over again. I don't know where we go in life from here."

Though Joshua's treatment for leukemia would end, his relationship with the disease would not. There was the immediate concern about whether the cancer was truly gone. When December 21 hit, it would be the first time since he was diagnosed that he was completely off chemotherapy. To me it felt like the first time a trapeze artist works with no net below him. Up until that point, we always had something to fall back on. The drugs were awful to be sure, but we were confident they were doing their job. But now there was no safety net; there was only the question of whether Joshua's body would continue to perform as it was supposed to.

The statistics say that if a child is going to relapse, it's most likely to happen inside the first year of going off chemotherapy. For that reason the good docs at Vanderbilt Children's Hospital would still watch Joshua closely during that first year. He would still go to the clinic every four weeks for blood tests and to make sure everything was just right. I remember those days, every four weeks, of standing on the emotional tightrope, slowly putting one step in front of the other, praying and worrying in the back of my mind that something would cause us to slip from the precarious position in which we'd found ourselves.

The anxiety for me didn't stop there. I worried about long-term psychological effects for Joshua and for us. Would he remember this? How would it affect his growth and development? A study going on right now is trying to determine if children who have had childhood cancers have a greater percentage of obesity, heart disease, and even learning disorders.

Also, because of all the drugs running in and out of his system during these three years, Joshua will be susceptible to other kinds of cancer as he grows. He'll be visiting the oncology department at least once a year until he's eighteen years old. It all added up to a tremendous amount of anxiety threatening to seriously impede what should have been a momentous celebration.

Anxious

I was a worried father, and I felt bad about that. Christians aren't supposed to worry; it's bad form. Jesus tells us not to worry about stuff like clothes or food because we have a foundation of trust in God as our provider.

Paul elaborated on the Christian response to worry in Philippians 4:6 saying: "Don't worry about anything, but in everything, through prayer and petition with thanksgiving, let your requests be made known to God." Peter, too, got in on the act in 1 Peter 5 urging his readers to "cast all their cares upon the Lord because He cares for them" (v. 7). So you've got two pillars of the early church and the Son of God Himself beating the same drum. It's pretty clear that God does not want His children to be filled with anxiety. That doesn't mean I couldn't rationalize my own worry.

After all, we had plenty to worry about. And one could certainly make the argument that there's a thin line between being anxious and being prepared. Don't responsibility and worry sort of hold hands? Shouldn't we plan for retirement?

Shouldn't we have life insurance? Shouldn't we think about the future? Where do you draw the line between responsibility and anxiety? And while we're at it, why would God be so concerned about His kids' anxiety?

Perhaps part of the reason is why we don't want our own children to worry. They're kids, and as such it shouldn't be their job to worry about whether or not there's going to be milk in the fridge in the morning. When our children live anxiety-free lives, it gives us as parents a great deal of joy in being able to provide what they need. But our lack of anxiety also communicates something to those outside the faith.

When we live with a lack of anxiety about the future, even in those tightrope kind of times, we communicate the truth that our God is indeed worthy of our trust. We don't fret over the future because He holds it in His hands. We don't wring our hands in worry because we know He's charting the course. That sort of confidence invites others into it, those longing for something different from life without a net.

Sounds great, right? The problem is the same in this area as with most things. It's easy to talk and write about, but when it comes right down to it, it's a lot more difficult than we think. Sounds simple—just make your requests to God and don't be anxious. But I found myself still with a rapidly beating heart and visions of an uncertain future when I finished praying. That's a far cry from what Paul said would happen in Philippians.

Peace

Paul urged us as followers of Jesus to be anxious for nothing but instead to pray. And the effect of that, according to him, is this: "And the peace of God, which surpasses every thought, will guard your hearts and minds in Christ Jesus" (Phil. 4:7). What a radical way to live. It's the kind of life, Paul admits, that doesn't really make sense. We shouldn't have this kind of peace, not with everything going on in our lives and the world. Not with a looming cancer threat. Not with job loss. Not with marriages falling apart. Not with all these and a host of other things going on in your life and mine. Paul talked about a peace that transcends understanding. A peace that we would be the first to acknowledge we don't really have a logical reason to have.

That sort of peace would have been nice, but that's not what I felt.

Then again, I think I had a misunderstanding of what peace really is. To say our nation is at peace means that we are currently not at war. In that definition peace is really just an absence of conflict. Not a bad goal to shoot for, whether in politics or in thinking about the future. I certainly would have settled for a lack of conflict about Joshua's finishing chemotherapy. But that's not really an adequate definition. Peace—real peace—is bigger than the absence of conflict.

What I mean is that a concept with a firm definition is defined by itself. To say that light is simply the opposite of darkness really doesn't do much to describe what light actually is. It only accounts for what it is not. If you really want to define light, you've got to talk in terms of lumens and brightness and glare and polarization. You can't just say that light is not dark. Likewise, you can't just say that peace is not conflict, though that may be true. Peace is bigger than that. It would have been bigger than that to Paul.

The Hebrew word for peace is *shalom*. It's a word used often in the Bible and even still in the vernacular of ethnic Jews today. It's a greeting when you see someone on the street and a closing when the conversation is over in some circles. But when you wish someone *shalom*, you're not just wishing them a lack of conflict. Sure, it would be nice for them to have a life outside of war, but the meaning of the word is bigger. The literal definition carries with it a sense of completeness.

In essence, that's what the state of *shalom* is—completeness. When you pass that word onto another, you are saying, "May you have a life that is whole." That wholeness is what Jesus is in the business of bringing to people like you and me because "wholeness" is what we've lost.

Lost

At least I felt like I had. Even on the best days, I walked around with a sense of brokenness. It's like I was shattered into pieces during Joshua's treatment, and now I'm glued back together, but I can't escape the rough edges. The ill-fitting pieces. I just feel . . . broken. I looked toward the future and felt aimless and directionless, like the pathway was somehow more dangerous than before.

Never before had I felt more like the coin Jesus described in Luke 15. It had fallen to the ground and inadvertently been swept away, lost in the cracks of the house. And it would have stayed lost if the woman who owned it had not gone to the trouble of finding it.

I was that coin. And Jesus was the great searcher, as He always is during times when we have lost our way. When the seeds of doubt, fear, and anxiety loom alongside the pathway and obstruct our view of Him. But like the woman in the story, He's not content to leave any of us in the cracks.

In Jesus' story anyone from the outside looking into the house of the searching woman would probably not join in the search because from the outside looking in they would not see the need. The coins in question here were ten denari. One denarius was equivalent to a quarter of a shekel, and the shekel was about a day's wage. She loses not a shekel but a quarter of a shekel.

In light of that, it is striking the effort the woman goes to in the search. She is incredibly deliberate and is willing to turn her house upside down to find it. She lights the lamp, she sweeps in the corner, and you can almost see the people looking in the window whispering that this woman is a little bit off. After all, you can understand her being upset at dropping some money, but the amount of effort she puts forth is not equivalent to what was lost. And if those neighbors looking in didn't think she was a little crazy before, how about the fact that she calls for a party when she finds the coin? She wants to host a celebration that would undoubtedly cost more than the amount she had found! She buys the hats, the streamers, the cake, the food—all to celebrate finding a sum equivalent to about seven dollars.

It's a lot of effort that leads to the inescapable conclusion: the woman highly valued what was lost. So does Jesus. His search reminds us that we are valued.

Mind you, however, that we aren't valued because we're valuable; we are valuable because we are valued by Him.

What does that search and the assignment of value have to do with *shalom*? It meant that even when my life felt incomplete and lost, even when circumstances were spiraling out of control, God valued me. And that brings peace. Real peace.

It brings wholeness. It brings completeness. If God values me, then I am in want for nothing else. I can live in shalom because of Him. It is as if Jesus were saying, "Please understand the value you have. Now respond by living in the freedom of wholeness."

Gospel

The gospel is about wholeness. It's about fractured, broken people being the gift of life through the life of another. In Christ we become complete and whole people—people who are in want for nothing.

Consider the amazing truth Paul expressed in Ephesians 1 when he said that we have been blessed in Christ with every spiritual blessing. Or again in Romans 8 that we will be given all things in Christ. Or back to Ephesians when he talked about the truly mind-boggling concept of inheritance.

In Ephesians 1:13–19, Paul used the word "inheritance" twice. The first occurs in verse 14: "He is the down payment of our inheritance, for the redemption of the possession, to the praise of His glory."

Paul talked about the Holy Spirit as earnest money. If you've ever bought a house, you know that you have to put down some earnest money as part of the contract. The earnest money isn't the full amount, but it's the amount of money you have to forfeit if you back out of the contract. To Paul, the Holy Spirit's indwelling presence is like earnest money. It's a deposit given to us by God that makes us sure He will uphold His end of the deal. It makes us sure that He will carry us onto completion, and we will receive our whole inheritance.

So what is that inheritance? We could say it's heaven, eternity, mansions, streets of gold, no more tears, and all the other stuff heaven brings along with it. But ultimately, I think you have to say the inheritance is the thing which makes heaven so heavenly—our inheritance is God. It's knowing Him fully and completely. That's what makes heaven so good, and that is what's waiting for us. The fact that God is giving us the greatest of all gifts, namely Himself, should bring us closer and closer to that sense of completeness.

But Paul wasn't done.

If we skip down to verse 18, this is what we find: "I pray that the perception of your mind may be enlightened so you may know what is the hope of His calling, what are the glorious riches of His inheritance among the saints, and what is the immeasurable greatness of His power to us who believe."

Do you see the difference? In this verse "inheritance" isn't talking about God or heaven; it's talking about us. We are the inheritance. So who is inheriting us? Who is waiting for us? Who considers us so valuable? God. We are God's inheritance.

It's unfathomable to think about what Christ did on the cross, that He bought something for us, but He also bought something for God. Jesus secured both our inheritances, and now God waits in expectation to fully inherit His. And God's inheritance? That's us.

Not only do we have an inheritance stored up for us, but we are of such value to the Creator that we are stored up for Him to the praise of His glory. This is a good reminder to me as gas prices are high, the economy is down, and jobs are in question; . . . but we are nonetheless rich in God. And maybe He's rich in us, too. The gospel reminds us that we are absolutely and completely whole. Complete. In Christ.

Is it any wonder, then, that in virtually all of his letters, Paul's greetings to the followers of Jesus consisted of two words: "grace" and "peace." Perhaps he chose those two words because they represent the gospel well. We are the beneficiaries of the lavish grace of God in Christ. And because of the gospel of Jesus, we are whole. We are complete. We lack nothing in Him. Now that's *shalom*.

Whole

That's what Paul was talking about. It wasn't just a lack of conflict; peace is about believing that we are truly valuable; and because we are, God is for us. No matter what my anxieties and worries were about the future, I could have completeness in Christ.

The truth was that I was anxious because of the fear of what I would lack in the future, over the disparity between how things are and how we wish they would be. But when we present our requests to God, through prayer and supplication with thanksgiving, we are reminded that He has and will continue to make us whole people.

That doesn't mean we'll get exactly what we think is the best thing for us. It certainly doesn't mean that our lives will be trouble free in the future. But it does mean we can count on the fact that God will give us what we need for each day. He's not going to leave us lacking.

Before everything happened with Joshua, long before the days of chemotherapy and heartache and loss, I used to wonder if I would have the strength to undergo severe testing of my faith. And truth be told, I wasn't sure.

And you know what? I'm still not.

But I have come to believe that because God has valued us so much and because He is interested in making us whole and complete people blessed with every spiritual blessing in Christ, we can count on the grace we need from Him when we need it.

When I woke up on October 18, 2006, I had no idea what was waiting for me. And consequently, I had no idea that the Lord had given me an extra measure of grace for that day. But by faith I believe that whatever happens in the future, the Lord will be faithful to dole out what I need when I need it. Enough grace to continue to put one foot in front of the other. That brings a sense of wholeness not only because we lack nothing now but because we believe, by His grace, that we will lack nothing we need in the future. That kind of grace can keep you walking, even if your walk becomes a limp.

Chapter 14

Limp

Party

Chick-fil-A is closed on Sundays. But when we began to think about where to have a party to celebrate Joshua's end to chemotherapy, we could think of no better place to have it than the restaurant we had eaten at so many times over the past three and a half years. How many times had Joshua sat there and looked through the glass at the play area? How many times had we tried to cheer him up as we explained to him that those play places were giant petri dishes? I picked up the owner's business card from the counter of our local restaurant and made a call. They could not cook the chicken, but they would provide the space. More importantly, they would provide the playground, even though the party was on Sunday. And there was yet another small reminder of the goodness of God.

On December 20, 2009, I watched my son put his last chemotherapy in his mouth, and I wasn't alone. My beautiful wife, Jana, pregnant with another little boy, stood looking on. Joshua's sister, Andi Hope, watched, too, though she didn't understand much of what was going on. About a hundred other people were there, packed into the eating area of our local Chick-fil-A. There were balloons and a huge sheet cake. There were scores of children and adults with tears in their eyes. My parents flew in from Texas to be at the party.

Finally, after more than three years, Joshua was going to play in the playground. The one where all the germs were. Heck, he might not even wash his hands afterwards.

He didn't chew up the pill; he stopped doing that a while back. He was a big boy now, so he took it down with a swallow of Coke. And then he played. Hard. He came out of that playground with his hair matted to his face and the back of his neck. And then, after a couple of hours, we did the strangest thing—we went home. And that was it.

The next morning I got up and went to work. Joshua and Andi watched PBS for half an hour and had breakfast. That night we continued to make preparations for our third child that would join us at home within a couple of weeks. Life goes on, I guess.

And yet it doesn't go on. I remembered walking out of the house on the cold morning of December 21 and driving to work. People drove past me. Then they walked past me at work. At the store. At restaurants. I remember thinking how amazing it was that our life had changed so much and yet the world kept right on spinning around us. Everything was the same, but everything was different. At least we were. Pain has a way of doing that to you. Like it or not, any experience like cancer affects you. Wounds you. Changes you. Life is different, and nothing is unaffected, especially not your relationship with Jesus. Your faith changes dramatically, sometimes for the good and sometimes for the bad. But make no mistake, it's different.

Walk

In reflection I found the Bible putting words to my experience. I resonated greatly with a single word in Scripture that is used to describe our life of faith. Growing up in church, I had always heard about my "personal relationship with Jesus Christ." It's a fine phrase, and I understand the meaning behind it. It means that we have more than a casual acquaintanceship with Jesus; that it's a relationship. And like any relationship it can be deep or shallow. It needs to be nurtured. We also find that the relationship is personal. We don't enter into it because of our association with a group or because we have a membership card. We come into it because something has happened to us individually, as persons. There's only one problem with the "personal relationship" phrase, if indeed you can call it a problem: it's not in the Bible. When the Bible describes how we interact with Jesus, we don't find the term anywhere in its pages. The Bible never talks about a "personal relationship with Christ." Sure, the ideas are there, but the terminology is absent. Instead, when the Bible talks about what we have with Jesus, we find a single word: *walk*.

Isn't it interesting that this is the word the Bible uses? The prophet Micah said that walking humbly with God is what is required of man. Paul framed his entire letter of Ephesians with the liberal usage of the word. It was the defining characteristic of the mysterious character of Enoch who didn't experience death. It certainly hit home with me because the last several years felt like a walk.

Sometimes those steps come easily. We've all been in seasons of life where it felt more like a run than a walk, where it seems like every moment we are experiencing the presence of God in an almost tangible way. That's not what the last three and half years felt like, though. Instead, our walk with God felt like we were trudging through quicksand or that our steps had virtually stopped. Most every step was an effort—a conscious choice to put one foot in front of the other. Our walk felt more like a struggle.

Struggle

Struggle is an intrinsic part of Christianity.

Now you can take that last statement a couple of ways, and they're both correct. Those who walk deeply with the Lord know what struggle is because they struggle daily to say yes to godliness and no to ungodliness. It's that simple.

The Christian life is about struggle because we know that walking with Jesus isn't like climbing a mountain. It's not that you earn levels of spiritual maturity through hard work until someday you get to a point in your life when you "arrive." In fact, those people who have walked longer and more deeply with Jesus would likely testify that their struggle with sin does not decrease but increase with time. The reason is that as you draw closer to Jesus, you see just how much remains inside of you that must be conformed to His image.

We encounter another sort of struggle as Christ followers if we want to walk deeply with God. And this struggle may be at least as difficult, if not more so, than the other one; for in this arena of struggle, God Himself is our opponent. In retrospect, that's sort of what our journey in and through cancer felt like much of the time. It felt like we were treading water, trying to keep our heads above water, pumping our legs and our arms in an effort to hang onto faith. We would cry out to the Lord, and though we now know and gratefully accept that His hidden hand was actually in that water holding us up, in the moment it felt absent. And when we did feel God's presence, it often seemed more like a fight than an embrace. Given those feelings, a vivid passage of Scripture gives us insight into what it means to wrestle with God, and it's found in Genesis 32:22–31. It's the climactic moment in the life of Jacob, son of Isaac, son of Abraham.

Jacob

That passage reveals an instance in Jacob's life when he was camped alongside the Jabok River. He was going to go across in the morning, and he would meet his long-estranged brother Esau there. Jacob was scared of the encounter. But as the passage reveals, Esau wasn't the only one who was waiting for Jacob.

Let's make no pretense about what has led to this moment. This is not an instance of poor, poor Jacob, just trying to cross a river. This is the climactic moment in the life of a shifty, scheming, deceptive man. And he's been that way for a long time.

Jacob was a twin; his brother Esau was born mere moments before he was, and Jacob came out grabbing his older brother's heel. That's how he got the name "Jacob." The same Hebrew root is found in the verb meaning "to take by the heel." However, that same root also means "to deceive." And this description turned out to be an accurate one.

The boys grew, and Jacob grew to be manipulative and self-serving. As the older brother, Esau was assumed to have the primary blessing of the family—the birthright. And yet Jacob took advantage of Esau's extreme hunger one day and convinced his brother to sell him the birthright over a bowl of lentil stew.

Jacob's deceptive nature surfaced again when his father, Isaac, was dying. When Isaac was about to give his older son, Esau, his blessing, Jacob deceived his father. See, Esau was a hairy dude, so Jacob covered himself with animal skins and convinced his father that he was Esau. So he stole the blessing right out from under him, but this time his deviousness was a threat to him. It was the last straw, and Esau was mad enough to kill his brother. So Jacob left and went to live with his uncle Laban.

Despite the whole fleeing-from-home-under-threat-of-his-life thing, Jacob's self-service and deception had worked out pretty well up to that point. Sure, he had to leave home, but he left with a birthright and a blessing, all because he was willing to look out for number one. And he continued to do that in his relationship with Uncle Laban. Over the next two decades or so, Jacob deceived his way into gaining a tremendous amount of wealth for himself, even going so far as manipulating the color of newly born goats. So when Jacob finally left Laban, he left as a con man who had fleeced yet another person out of his stuff. But all that was about to change because in Genesis 32, Jacob had run out of places to go, and so he was going back home. And back home was where his robbed, deceived, and angry brother Esau was. Suddenly Jacob was confronted with a crisis situation.

Though an outsider looking in at Jacob's life might have observed that Jacob was canny but unscrupulous, always in any situation for his own good, there was something else happening behind the scenes. The sovereign hand of God was at work in Jacob's life, whether or not he knew it. God had decided long before Jacob's deception that the blessing would pass through him. He decided long before Jacob that he would marry Rachel. God had been directing events and sovereignly working for years and years through the major events of Jacob's life like birth order as well as the seemingly insignificant ones like the number of spots on a goat. And up until this point, God was content to allow Jacob to think that he was responsible for it all. But no longer. God had been engineering this night for a long time. He had been engineering this moment of crisis for Jacob.

That's a common thread for all of us. The statistics say that there was about a one in 440,000 chance that Joshua would have leukemia. But he got it. You just happened to work in an industry that was hit hard by an economic downturn, and though you thought there was a small chance of losing your job, it happened. Your marriage was once rock solid, impenetrable by things like pornography, bitterness, and loneliness, and yet there you are. In all of these circumstances, there is at least the moment when you sit back and marvel at what has happened. And the thought lingering in your head is simply: *What were the chances?* You were just minding your own business, and then one day . . .

Then one day you come to a moment of absolute crisis. You hear that your dad has terminal cancer. The relationship you had placed all your hope for the future in ends. You lose your job or your scholarship. Your life isn't where you thought it would be. It's a moment of crisis. And in that moment you realize that you don't have anywhere to turn. No one can really help you. Oh, we say that we live by faith and trust God, and yet throughout the vast majority of our lives we have, in practicality, the same life philosophy as Jacob: self-reliance and manipulation of circumstances to our advantage. We trust in our ability to interview, our ability to network, our ability to form relationships. We trust in our earning potential, our insurance plans, and our trust funds. We trust ourselves. But in a moment of crisis, in a true moment of crisis, we come face-to-face with our own inability and utter powerlessness to affect any real change in our lives. We are confronted with our own mortality, that our days are as dust, and that we can't do anything about it.

That's where Jacob was, and that's where we find ourselves on diagnosis day. Or pink slip day. Or the day the papers are served. That's why earlier in the chapter Jacob made a last-ditch effort to send his family ahead of him. He had come to this moment of this crisis, and he knew that he might well die because of his past of deception. He had nothing left—no plan B or clever tactic. So he started to pray, as we all do in those moments. As the saying goes, there are no atheists in foxholes. Neither are there many atheists in emergency rooms. And in that moment the figure that stepped out of the shadows was much more imposing than Jacob's brother Esau.

Engage

What must have gone through Jacob's mind when he looked out and saw the man in front of him in Genesis 32? Was it fear? Was it panic? Did he consider making a deal with him as he had so many times in the past? Did he wonder how he was going to connive his way out of this one? Maybe all of those things, or maybe we know even more specifically what it felt like. It's the same thing you and I have felt or will feel when we have the watershed moment of clarity as we turn around to the path behind us and see that God had been directing our steps all along. We walk through our lives casually, and yet the loving, redemptive hand of God is always at work—positioning, moving, placing—and it's incredibly humbling. But it's also uncomfortable when we look before us and see the shadowy figure of God waiting there. And we know then we can't go any farther in life until we confront Him. He has engineered this moment of crisis for us. And He wants to wrestle.

Let me say it again: God wants to wrestle. Indeed, that is the reason, at least in many cases, He brings us to the moment of crisis. In that moment He's the one standing in the shadows. Not chance. Not bad luck. God.

But why?

That's a good question. Why does God want to wrestle? Why did He want to wrestle Jacob? If He is behind this, if He orchestrates these moments, then there must be something of value in the wrestling match.

Perhaps it is this: you can go only so far in a relationship without wrestling. That's certainly how it has been in my relationships. I have acquaintances I'm cordial enough with. We know stuff about each other, where each other is from, what we do for a living, which college football teams we each like—stuff like that. We get together and hang out. We go to movies. We have dinner. We laugh and carry on.

Yet in those relationships, which I'm sure you have plenty of, too, don't you wonder just how deep your association with that person is? I compare those many kinds of acquaintances with the handful of real, deep friendships that exist in my life. And there is a marked difference.

The truth is that some of those friends are actually harder to be around than the acquaintances. Ironically it's because those friends know me more, not less, than the acquaintances. And because they do, there is little time for idle chatter and chitchat in a lot of cases. When a relationship progresses past movies and playlists and an occasional dinner, it starts to deepen. But it's not until you begin to wrestle in that relationship that a truly deep relationship forms.

It's not until you have had arguments, sat through loss, and had difficult discussions about insecurities and doubts and fears that you become truly intimate with another person. Perhaps this is at least in part why many marriages fail. We think we know a person when we get married only to wake up the next day and realize, much to our chagrin, that we really don't know that person at all. To truly know and be intimate with another, you have to sit together when there is no money. When the casket is being brought down the aisle. When the future is uncertain.

A relationship can only proceed to true intimacy when there has been some wrestling. Through conflict and the resolving of that conflict we truly learn about each other. You have to sit through arguments, sickness, tragedy, misunderstandings, as well as trivial happiness; and when you do, you are bonded with someone else. Because there's no other way to be except close when you wrestle. When you wrestle, you smell someone's sweat. Your face is pressed against the other's chest. You are locked in combat, and the closeness is by its nature uncomfortable.

Jacob knew all about God. He must have. He must have heard stories about this God and His covenant from his grandpa Abraham and his father Isaac. Maybe his daddy had told him about the day when Grandpa took him up the mountain with a knife and wood but no sacrifice, how he strapped him down, how the tears filled his eyes, and then how he heard the voice from on high. He knew about God.

But on the other hand, he was a classic avoider of conflict. He was much more prone to manipulation than he was to hashing things out. When the going got tough, Jacob was not someone of perseverance but someone who cut and ran. He ran from his dad. He ran from his brother. He ran from his uncle. And so do we.

We run from the difficulties of Scripture when we encounter them. We hide behind "God's will" when we pray for things and they don't happen. We take notes about five ways to have our best life now. We drown ourselves in church activities and Bible studies. And in our relationships we hide behind the pretense of "I'm fine" when the struggles wage within us. We avoid. But God wants to wrestle. He wanted to wrestle Jacob, and He wants to wrestle us because we reach a point when God will not allow us to live in shallowness any longer. When the moment of crisis comes and God steps out of the shadows, we've got a choice: do we run and live forever in the shallow end of God; or do we engage in the sweaty, hard, arduous, uncomfortable work of wrestling?

Jacob engaged (see Gen. 32:24). And we engage. We battle. We battle emotionally, through prayer, through doubt, through questions. We battle, and the sweat of God rubs off on us. Spit from our mouths drips onto His chest. And in the throws of that battle, with the sweat and the tangled arms and the throbbing leg muscles, here is the question from the mouth of God that gets whispered over and over in our ears: "Do you believe?"

That question, friends, is at the core of everything. It's at the core of our being. It's at the core of our relationships. It's at the core of our world. The issue of trust is absolutely paramount, and for that issue God has brought us, and Jacob, to this point of struggle.

We fool ourselves into thinking that belief and trust are related to some issues in our lives, but they are not. They are all-encompassing. We think temptation is about the will; it's not. It's about faith. It's about faith that God's power is strong enough in you to say no, and it's about having the faith that says Jesus is better than that momentary temptation. We think our life situations are about choosing the wisest, most beneficial course of action; they're really about faith. They're about faith that God's way is better. We think that eating is about fulfilling our desires; it's not. It's about faith that our bodies really are a temple of the Holy Spirit and should be treated as such. And we think the difficult moments of our lives are just about hanging on and getting through them; they're not. They're about trust. They're about trusting in the abiding wisdom, love, and care of God who is directing our paths.

That's what the wrestling match is over; it's about faith. It's about trust. And so the question comes over and over again as we desperately try to hang onto the fabricated notion that we are in control and are the charters of our own destiny. "Do you trust me?"

Trust is so important that God will fight us for it.

Name

But Jacob—Jacob who had only trusted in himself, who had trust in his ability to make things happen, his ability to manipulate situations, his ability to handle his own life—Jacob was not ready to give up. Even in the throes of the wrestling match, he was hanging onto his own ability to control his own life. He had one last-ditch effort in his mind. And so he held on and brazenly told God, "I won't let go until you bless me." I've done the same thing, and maybe you have, too. Even in those moments of crisis, when we know we can do nothing to help ourselves, we are still hell-bent on our own self-preservation. We hold with white knuckles to our own ability to fix things in our lives. Jacob was still the fixer, even as he was engaged in a wrestling match with God. It was as if he was hanging onto his ability to make that blessing happen, and then God did something that changed everything. He asked one, simple question:

"What is your name?"

That's a huge question, for to the Hebrews the name was much more than someone's title. The name was the essence of the person's identity. And Jacob had lived up to his moniker—he was a deceiver. Can you see the light go out of Jacob's eyes with the question? He's straining with exhaustion, holding on with all his might, when suddenly his entire life comes into focus with just one question. With this question God forced Jacob to examine the way he had been living his life, how he had been always committed to doing his best for himself. And now, caught in a struggle he could not win, Jacob had to own up to who he really was.

His arms must have felt weak. Maybe his head started to droop. In shame and frustration he felt his resolve leave him, and he had to answer honestly, maybe for the first time in his life: "I am a deceiver."

This is what happens in the battle for our trust. As God fights for our faith, we are forced to reckon with our own lack of faith. We are forced to realize the path of selfishness and self-preservation we've been on. We are forced to spit out our own name when we are securely held within His grip. Through our clenched teeth, we hear the truth of who we are:

Liar.
Addict.
Manipulator.
Doubter.
Deceiver.

What a hopeless situation! We are brought to bear with the truth of ourselves in the midst of that painful embrace. We do not like what we see. The weight of ourselves threatens to crush us. But then the astounding happens to us as it did to Jacob:

The One who named the stars in the sky whispers a new name in our ear.

Jacob emerged from the struggle with a new title, but more than that, with a new sense of who he was (see Gen. 32:28). He wasn't the deceiver any longer; he was Israel. And Israel means something much, much different from Jacob. Israel means, "God contends." Jacob means self-sufficient. Israel is a reminder of human frailty. Jacob means counting on yourself. Israel means trusting in God. Jacob is a commentary on human ability; Israel is an expression of God's power. Jacob went forth from that moment—from that struggle—no longer the self-sufficient one with trust in himself but as one whose faith was in God to persevere. And that name became the name by which the people of God are still known.

The people who were threatened by nations in the Old Testament and yet God led them through. The people who were caught in slavery and yet God led them through. The people who were caught on one side of the Red Sea and yet God led them through. The people who were disobedient and then sent into exile, but God led them through. And then ultimately, the people who gave birth to the One who knew what it was truly like to absolutely trust in God.

The same can happen for us. We enter the wrestling match with God so sure of everything only to find our world crumbling within His grip. We are forced to reckon with who we really are, in all our doubt, fear, and selfishness; but God doesn't leave us there. He's not just fighting for the sake of fighting; He's fighting for our trust, and when He's got it, He wants to give us a new name, too.

Son.

Daughter.

Treasured possession.

Inheritance.

Saint.

Brother and sister of the King of the universe.

Limp

Jacob left the wrestling match that night with a new name, but that's not all. The text says that God reached down and touched Jacob on his hip socket. Jacob was marked by the struggle with a limp. Isn't that interesting.

If the biblical language for our relationship with God is framed in terms of a walk, Jacob limped. As he walked forward, his walk was marked by the struggle. Such is the case with all who struggle with God. Coming out of cancer or whatever crisis situation precipitated the struggle, we all limp—we emotionally, spiritually, and sometimes even physically hobble along the journey of life.

We have struggled with God, and we have come away from that wrestling match changed. Wounded somehow. Broken. We continue to walk with the Lord, but our gate is awkward because of what we've been through. Jacob limped, too, and I wonder how he felt about it.

It must have been inconvenient at times. It must have been humbling, too. Surely there were times when he looked at his cane, felt the pain of the old wound, and wondered if it were really worth it. But I suspect that in Jacob's life, and in ours moving forward, the way in which we walk with God will do more than just remind us of the past. It will surely do that; I'm sure there won't be many times when the past years of leukemia will be far from mind. But I also think that limping along really isn't a bad way to walk.

The limp, both for Jacob and for us, is a permanent reminder of human frailty and divine power. This, friends, is the essence of trust—it is a knowledge of our own inability and an acknowledgment that we serve a mighty God.

We wrestle with God over the trust of our lives. And we don't come out of that struggle unchanged. Our walk with Him is forever altered. We come out limping, but that limp is a reminder of what faith is really all about. So we limp forward, . . . but we do so in faith. And as we do, we take comfort in this—our traveling companion knows the wrestling match, too.

Jesus knows how to wrestle. And wrestle He did that night in the garden. He wrestled with the cross that was coming. He wrestled with what had been set before Him. And in that wrestling match, when Jesus was asked the same question of belief, through drops of blood He looked to the sky and said, "I trust you." And after that wrestling match, He was marked, too, except His marks were holes in His hands and His side.

I guess we would look like a ragtag bunch on the road together—Jesus with His "holey" side and all of us with our canes, all walking together down the road of life. But someday . . . someday, when we get to the end of the journey and we all compare wounds from our time on Earth, and we realize that those were really light and momentary struggles in the light of eternity with God, we'll celebrate together that we are loved by a God who loves us enough to wrestle us for our faith, and that our limps and wounds remind us that He is, in any circumstance, ultimately, divinely, lovingly, abidingly able.

Jesus will show off His own marks. We'll hold up our canes. Then we'll all put them aside—Enoch, Abraham, Moses, David, Jacob, Paul, and all the rest who have been crippled on the journey. We'll put them aside because we're finally home. And it will be time for dinner.

Until then we continue to walk with God. To limp with God. That limp, the brokenness that will go with us until the end, doesn't just mark us as people who have had a child with cancer. It's a mark that reminds us of the God who is worthy of our trust. He's the One we have wrestled, and yet He is the One who has sustained us. Even now.

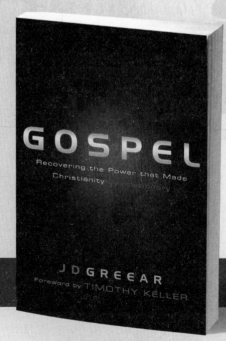